Cacti,
Succulents
Bromelia

A Wisley Gardening Companion

Cacti, Succulents and Bromeliads

CLIVE INNES AND
BILL WALL

Cassell

The Royal Horticultural Society

THE ROYAL HORTICULTURAL SOCIETY

Cassell Educational Limited
Wellington House, 125 Strand
London WC2R 0BB
for the Royal Horticultural Society

This compilation copyright © Cassell/The Royal
  Horticultural Society 1995

Cacti copyright © Clive Innes 1987, 1992
Succulents copyright © Clive Innes 1989
Air Plants and Other Bromeliads copyright © Bill Wall
  1988 and Clive Innes 1994

First published 1995

British Library Cataloguing in Publication Data
A catalogue record for this book is available from the
British Library

ISBN 0–304–32076–5

Photographs by John Glover, Clive Innes, Photos
Horticultural, Peter Stiles and Bill Wall. Line drawings
by Maureen Holt and Mike Shoebridge

Phototypesetting by RGM Typesetting, The Mews,
Birkdale Village, Southport, England

Printed in Hong Kong by Wing King Tong Co. Ltd.

Front cover: Parodia herteri, has flowers in bright or pale
shades of reddish purple
Page 1: Adenium obesum, also known as desert rose
Page 2: A mixed collection of cacti and succulents,
dominated by the large round 'pincushions' of
Echinocactus grusonii
Back cover: Aloinopsis schooneesii flowers in late summer
and autumn and is dormant in winter

Contents

Foreword

It gives me particular pleasure to introduce the Society's Wisley Gardening Companion to *Cacti, Succulents and Bromeliads.* This volume amalgamates three more of the popular and long-established Wisley Handbooks: *Cacti, Succulents* and *Air Plants and Other Bromeliads.*

When I first joined the Society I grew cacti and succulents in my office – they were the only plants I thought would tolerate the sun streaming in during summer months and the hot, dry, centrally heated conditions that prevailed in winter. I had the joy of seeing them produce their brilliant flowers as they thrived where many other indoor plants would fail.

In many ways, cacti and other succulent plants and also bromeliads are ideal house plants. They are tough and easy to care for – provided, that is, they are given good light, the gritty compost that ensures sharp drainage and are not over-watered. Their shapes vary enormously, but invariably they have a sculptural quality which makes them so different from other groups of plants. The flowers, when they appear, are often spectacular and always exciting, partly because their flamboyance is so unexpected.

Many bromeliads develop large rosettes of colourful leaves. The central 'urn' will need to be filled with water from time to time, but otherwise they are remarkably resilient. In contrast, air plants, also part of the bromeliad family, appear very different. Their tufts of silvery foliage can be attached to pieces of driftwood to make simple, abstract arrangements which merely require regular misting with water to keep them going.

A full account of how to grow these fascinating plants is given in the following pages. The many pictures and descriptions, I am confident, will encourage you to seek out the more unusual species as you pursue what I know to be a fascinating hobby.

Gordon Rae
Director General
The Royal Horticultural Society

An Echinopsis cultivar, one of the many beautiful plants of the genus which flower readily during the day

Cacti

—— CLIVE INNES ——

Opuntia microdasys, one of the most frequently grown
species of this extensive genus

Above: *Rhipsalis baccifera*, a tropical epiphyte with flowers followed by small white berries (see p.40)
Below: *Astrophytum ornatum* belongs to a small but popular genus of desert cacti (see p.45)

Introduction

The last few years have seen the introduction of many new species of cacti. Exciting discoveries have been made, especially in more remote areas of Central and South America. Some of these have reached our shores and can be obtained in seed form or perhaps as young plants. A number of specialist nurseries propagate, distribute and encourage interest in cacti, while enthusiasts meet regularly throughout the country under the auspices of the British Cactus and Succulent Society. There have also been several reclassifications of the cactus family by botanists in Europe and the USA, resulting in name changes both to genera and to species. The titles used here reflect the most recent changes (1994).

Over 200 genera are represented in the Cactaceae, involving numerous species, varieties and forms, the majority of which are available in cultivation. Like all succulent plants, cacti are very adaptable and may be used in the home or greenhouse and even as garden plants. Remembering their natural habitat – at one extreme the harsh semi-arid expanses of desert, and at the other the jungles where many well known and popular species grow epiphytically* in company with orchids and bromeliads – this vast family is indeed unique.

The need for conservation is now widely recognized and cacti seem to be particularly threatened. In the name of progress and economic development, whole regions of desert and jungle have been cleared of their plant populations to make room for food production, highways and townships; the indiscriminate collection of wild plants by man has led to further devastation of natural habitats. These areas must be preserved wherever possible. Equally essential is the conservation of cacti in botanical collections, both public and private, and in general cultivation.

Cacti are succulents in the accepted sense of the word, although there might be a few exceptions whose structure does not merit the term. Their ability to store moisture and food enables them to survive and they have adjusted themselves fully to their environment. Desert rainfall is sporadic and invariably fierce when it

*An epiphyte is a plant which grows on another without being nourished by it and is not a parasite.

comes, sometimes even flooding the flat open spaces, although the waters quickly subside because of the porous nature of the ground. During this brief period the plants have to take up and store nourishment until the next storm, perhaps many months or even years ahead. These peculiarities of the natural habitat of cacti should always be borne in mind when considering their cultural requirements.

I hope here to provide the reader with a better understanding of these exotic and bizarre plants, explaining their origins and characteristics, suggesting guidelines for their cultivation and propagation and finally describing a representative selection of the plants available to the gardener.

Cacti and succulents in a greenhouse, including the tall branching *Cereus hildmannianus* 'Monstrosus' (see p.46), various columnar cacti and the variegated agave

Geographical Distribution

All cacti are native to North and South America. In many other parts of the tropics and sub-tropics, certain species have become naturalized and been mistaken for true natives of South Africa, Australia and southern Europe. A handful of cactus species, mainly epiphytic, have been encountered as wild plants in east Africa and Madagascar, but whether they are truly endemic or merely escapes which have gradually adapted to the prevailing conditions has not been decided.

The cactus sphere extends from southern Canada through to central, western and southern regions of the United States, then to Mexico, Central America, the West Indian islands and all South American countries right down to the southernmost tip of Argentina. Many species, and for that matter genera, differ noticeably according to altitude, which ranges from sea level to elevations of over 16,000 ft (5,000 m).

Mexico has the greatest concentration of cacti. Temperatures and humidity vary considerably: on the Baja California, the Pacific coastal areas enjoy a warm comfortable climate, while regions bordering the Gulf of California are often oppressively hot. The Baja provides the habitat of some of the more uncommon *Echinocereus* and *Opuntia* species and of the creeping devil, *Stenocereus eruca* (the erstwhile *Machaerocereus eruca*), a plant unknown elsewhere. On the mainland in Sonora and Sinaloa are many different *Mammillaria*, *Echinocereus* and *Ferocactus*, together with occasional colonies of rarer genera such as *Peniocereus*. Perhaps the most dominating plant found here is *Pachycereus pringlei* and, along with *Carnegiea gigantea*, the huge saguaro (which is also a native of Arizona), it is truly spectacular.

From Chihuahua and Coahuila southwards are seen *Ariocarpus*, *Astrophytum*, *Thelocactus*, *Ancistrocactus* and *Lophophora*. The choice *Mammillaria plumosa* is located at altitudes of 6,500 ft (2,000 m). Further south on limestone cliffs in Hidalgo is the home of *Cephalocereus senilis*, one of the most distinctive Mexican cacti. Below Mexico City in the moist tropical forest zones of Chiapas, which extend through to Guatamala, Honduras and Costa Rica, the scene changes to reveal the first signs of epiphytic cacti – *Epiphyllum*, *Hylocereus*, *Disocactus*, *Selenicereus* and *Rhipsalis*. At

Stenocereus thurberi is a common inhabitant of Mexico and Arizona (see p.66)

the same time, on the more barren mountain slopes and often in close proximity to the forest, there are further species of *Opuntia* and columnar *Cereus* and some of the sprawling, trailing *Acanthocereus, Nyctocereus* and the like.

Dense rain forest is a feature of many parts of South America and the West Indies. Rare plants such as *Strophocactus wittii* can be discovered in the Amazon forests, while typical jungle cacti such as *Rhipsalis, Schlumbergera* and *Epiphyllum* are natives of Brazil, some genera also being represented in Peru, Chile and Ecuador. The West Indies contain a number of isolated examples of epiphytic cacti, mainly *Rhipsalis, Hylocereus, Selenicereus* and *Epiphyllum*.

South America, especially Ecuador, Peru, Chile and Brazil, has been explored by many important expeditions since 1979. Species of *Cleistocactus, Oroya* and *Neoporteria* from Peru have been discovered and introduced to cultivation in more recent years, adding to the examples already known of *Espostoa, Melocactus, Opuntia, Haageocereus* and many others. Ecuador is well represented by species of *Armatocereus* and the more columnar *Cleistocactus*.

Chile has almost a monopoly of certain genera – *Copiapoa, Neoporteria, Eulychnia* and *Neowerdermannia* to mention but a few. These occur at different elevations, from flat coastal plains to some of the higher rocky slopes of the Andes. The totally

Opuntia palmadora from Brazil, a rare member of a widespread genus

landlocked Bolivia is the home of *Gymnocalycium*, *Rebutia*, *Cleistocactus*, *Quiabentia* and others. Paraguay and Brazil share several genera, including *Parodia*, *Notocactus*, *Echinopsis*, *Melocactus* and *Discocactus*. Southern Brazil has been the source of some of the most exciting discoveries of cacti, among them species of a fairly new genus, *Uebelmannia*, *Discocactus horstii*, a charming miniature, and the outstanding *Coleocephalocereus*.

Northern Argentina, together with Uruguay, is the habitat of *Oreocereus*, *Gymnocalycium*, *Cleistocactus*, *Notocactus*, *Acanthocalycium* and *Lepismium*. In more southerly Argentina on the high mountain slopes of Patagonia are species of *Maihuenia*, a genus rarely encountered in cultivation which is related to *Opuntia*. In fact no genus is more widely distributed then *Opuntia*, which is found from southern Canada to southern Argentina.

In the West Indies, which have comparatively few genera, *Melocactus* is probably the commonest, the species often varying from one island to the other. Cuba appears to have the most and certainly the greatest number of different species of *Melocactus*, as well as *Dendrocereus* and *Leptocereus*.

Two genera, *Jasminocereus* and *Brachycereus*, are totally confined to the Galapagos Islands, which have for many years been a plant sanctuary. The species of *Opuntia* found there are among the most attractive in this vast genus.

17

Characteristics

All cacti are dicotyledons, that is, they have two seed leaves when they germinate, and all are perennial. With a few exceptions, they usually take one growing season, or often much longer, to mature to flowering stage.

The Cactaceae as a family have many distinguishing features which set them apart from any other form of plant life. The most prominent characteristic is the areole, a round or elongated cushion of felt, hair or wool on the plant stems or bodies. The areole actually incorporates two growing points: flower buds and 'branches' (if the species is one which offsets or 'branches') are produced from the upper one and spines (if the species has spination) develop from the lower one. In certain genera, particularly *Mammillaria*, these two growing points are well separated, but generally they are so close together as to appear almost united. In some epiphytic genera such as *Epiphyllum* and *Schlumbergera*, the areoles are very minute and difficult to locate.

The cephalium is a cap or crown formed terminally on certain columnar and sometimes globular cacti of flowering size, which becomes larger each year. It consists of densely packed woolly areoles or bristles (not spines). The flowers develop from the areoles hidden inside the cephalium.

Most epiphytic cacti are readily distinguishable. The flattish, leaf-like stems are an outstanding feature in *Epiphyllum*, *Disocactus* and *Weberocereus* and a few other genera. Some of these leaf-like cacti have either deep or shallow crenations or notches along the margins. In the genus *Schlumbergera* the leaf-like segments are oblong or rounded with slightly notched edges, or sometimes very obviously toothed as with the species once included under *Zygocactus*.

Other epiphytic types have rather different stem features. *Hylocereus*, which includes some species with the largest flowers in the Cactaceae, are climbing, clambering plants and generally have triangular stems with woody margins and a few stumpy hard spines. In all species, aerial roots develop sparsely along the stems and at the constrictions (points which denote where new growth starts). *Selenicereus*, also a climber with large nocturnal flowers, usually has numerous aerial roots. The elongated stems are

18

normally ribbed, sometimes with prominent projections at intervals along the ribs. The new growth can be 3, 4, 5 or 6-sided, but with maturity the stems become almost roundish.

Of all epiphytic cacti, the most difficult to determine and controversial are *Rhipsalis* and *Lepismium* and others of related genera. Botanically, *Lepismium* is identified by a sunken ovary in the stem margin. The stem varies greatly and is often 3-angled with a purplish red appearance and slightly undulating, at other times with rib-like formations or several branchlets developing from one point in whorls. All species have aerial roots and very pronounced areoles, but few, if any, spines.

Rhipsalis has fairly small, sometimes insignificant flowers. The stems are usually spineless, although a few species have soft bristles or hairs which can disappear with age. Without exception, they are of pendent habit with mostly elongated stems and branches, but they differ tremendously in form. Long slender pencil-shaped stems are typical of many, either in short sections or long growths to 3 ft (1 m) or more in length. Others have angular stems, pronouncedly triangular or with 5 to 7 distinct ribs. A few have leaf-like sections similar to *Epiphyllum* or *Schlumbergera*, often notched and occasionally with undulating margins. All have aerial roots and more or less obvious areoles.

Of the desert or semi-desert cacti (as opposed to the epiphytic cacti), the cerei are mostly columnar plants and fairly easy to recognize. The erect species are probably in the majority, although to give an overall characteristic would be impossible. Some are very heavily ribbed and spined, others only moderately so, and many are night-flowering. Some genera are of prostrate habit, for instance *Stenocereus eruca*, which in nature trails extensively and is viciously spined. *Heliocereus*, the sun cactus, has mainly 3 to 4-sided stems and is frequently semi-pendent, with startling orange, white or rich crimson flowers.

Mammillaria is one of the most popular and important genera and comprises a great number of diverse species which produce flowers of white through to rich purplish red. Mostly globular or slightly columnar, they may be solitary or clump-forming, normally with dense spines. The ribs are less noticeable than the tubercles or warts, which are mostly spirally arranged and encircling the body of the plant. Flowers are borne in the axils or angles of the tubercles from the upper part of the areoles, always appearing on the side of the plant and often in a complete circle.

The *Opuntia* include many species, some with pad-shaped sections of the stem, others cylindrical in shape. Several species are low-growing, with the stems and branches consisting of small, somewhat stunted, oval, round or elongated segments. All have areoles with small barbed bristles or hairs in clusters, a peculiarity of this group of cacti. These glochids, as they are known, can be irritating to the skin and are easily broken off.

The majority of cacti do not possess leaves. Some species of *Opuntia* and *Cereus* produce small fleshy leaves on new growth, but generally these soon drop off. The sole exception is *Pereskia*, which has non-succulent, invariably deciduous leaves. Plants are bushy, semi-erect or clambering, with large areoles and long spines. The flowers are among the most attractive of the Cactaceae, somewhat rose-like and cream, yellow or magenta.

Of the desert cacti, only a few are completely or partly spineless, or have the spines replaced by hairs or bristles, notably *Ariocarpus*, *Aztekium*, *Lophophora* and certain species of *Astrophytum*. Spines are undoubtedly a very important characteristic of cacti as a whole and can provide a guide to the identification of a genus or even species.

Most of the barrel-shaped or globular plant – *Ferocactus*, *Echinocactus*, *Parodia* and *Echinopsis* – have pronounced symmetrical ribs, some completely vertical, others spirally arranged. These may be widely spaced or quite close together. Occasionally, for instance in species of *Parodia*, they are so close and so densely covered with spines and hairs that it is almost impossible to appreciate the rib formation.

Flowers are, of course, the greatest feature of cacti. Although a very few have small uninteresting flowers, by far the majority produce beautiful blooms, sometimes up to 8 in. (20 cm) or more in diameter. Almost every colour is represented, apart from blue, and many are very fragrant, especially those opening at night. Nocturnal flowers last for only one night, usually appearing in late afternoon or evening and closing and withering soon after sunrise or during the early hours of the morning. Diurnal or daytime flowers may last for a number of days, some as many as four or five, although unfortunately a number are shortlived. However, these plants sometimes compensate by producing many flowers in succession over a period of weeks or even months.

Above left: *Schlumbergera truncata*, a parent of the well known Christmas cactus (see p.40)
Right: *Pereskia aculeata*, a climbing plant with true leaves and spectacular scented flowers (see p.65)
Below: *Echinocereus* species like this one produce large, colourful, long-lasting flowers

Cultivation

CACTI IN THE GREENHOUSE

In the northern hemisphere the greenhouse is the most convenient and reliable method of growing exotics, including cacti. It should be sound, strong and weatherproof, with a close-fitting roof so that no drips can damage the plants, and free of draughts but at the same time well ventilated to stimulate plant growth and discourage stagnation. The greenhouse should receive the maximum amount of light, which is the main natural requirement of cacti, and the glass should be kept clean. Some form of shading can be beneficial in summer when the sun is at its height. Heating depends on your choice of plants. A minimum temperature of 46°–50°F (8° to 10°C) is ample, unless really tropical species are being grown. However, with some of the supposedly temperamental cacti, such as species of *Melocactus* and *Discocactus*, the temperature should not fall below 59°F (15°C). Do not install any heating equipment which gives off harmful fumes.

If you want a mixed collection of semi-desert and epiphytic cacti, it is essential to segregate them. The former prefer as much light as possible, although not necessarily full sun. On the other hand, epiphytes, which come from forests, require protection from glaring sunlight and some shading, at least in the summer. A position under the greenhouse bench will suit many of the non-hanging basket kinds and in all cases one should avoid too bright a situation.

Watering is very important for cacti. In this respect it is advisable to know your plants and their pattern of growth, bearing in mind the fact that they experience prolonged drought and sudden rainstorms in their natural habitats. All cacti alternate between periods of growth, when they need water, and periods of dormancy, when they should normally be kept dry (or fairly dry in the case of many epiphytes) and cool. So first determine whether they grow and flower in winter or summer and then water accordingly – not forgetting a favourable temperature for those that are winter growers. With most of the desert cacti, watering can cease completely from early November to March.

How often should you water? When the soil is dry, water well and soak thoroughly, then wait until the soil is dry again before repeating. Plants can be watered from above in the normal way, but this should not be done in the heat of the day. Early in the morning is the best time, before the sun rises too high, or as late in the evening as possible, when temperatures have dropped and the plants are cooler. Do not leave cacti standing in water: complete and constant drainage is essential and waterlogging can be calamitous. Equally dangerous is to give small amounts of water every day or so, which prevents the plants using up their nourishment.

Soil is perhaps the most controversial aspect of cultivation and what one enthusiast finds satisfactory is not necessarily acceptable to another. However, the inclusion of grit or sharp sand in the soil mix cannot be too strongly recommended, for the mixture must be porous to enable aeration to play its part. Nutrients (see below) should be incorporated into the mixture and should be supplemented by later feeding in order to encourage and sustain growth and flowering. Many good composts are now commercially prepared and available from garden shops. Soilless composts can be easily adapted for the cultivation of cacti by adding small, sharp, washed grit, to make up a third or more of the total bulk. Most are manufactured with the appropriate nutrients included, but these may last for only a limited period of weeks or months depending on the absorption rate of the plant. Soil-based composts like John Innes no. 2 can give equally good results, although even with these it may be necessary to add more grit.

If you wish to mix your own compost and can obtain a really good uncontaminated loam, the following proportions should be used: 1 part good sterilized loam; 1 part well sifted, decomposed leafmould; 1 part sharp, gritty, washed sand; plus a sprinkling of slow-release fertilizer and ideally a little decomposed cow manure. Charcoal chippings may also be added to prevent souring of the soil. Some lime should be included for species from limestone habits (as indicated in the Directory, p. 34).

Nutrients will be absorbed only if the plant is growing well and has an efficient root system. Otherwise, if it looks dehydrated or unhealthy, it is best removed from the pot, examined for pest or rot, cleaned or cut to deal with the problem and then repotted before feeding starts again. There are very few fertilizers specifically designed for cacti, but most of the general fertilizers available contain nitrogen and potash which can be beneficial. It is wise to use fertilizers incorporating the essential trace elements of iron, magnesium, manganese, copper, boron and molybdenum, all of which play a part in producing the sort of plant to which the enthusiast aspires!

Cacti growing at the Frankfurt Palm Garden, with *Cephalocereus senilis* and the red-spined *Ferocactus cylindraceus* in front (see pp.46 and 54)

Liquid fertilizer or powdered fertilizer dissolved in water is particularly suitable for later feeding. As a general rule, cacti in the greenhouse should be fed in early April, about a week after emerging from dormancy, and then once a month until early October. Fertilizer should never be given during the dormant period.

The type of container to choose is a matter of taste. The critical factor is the material from which it is made, which affects the frequency of watering: clay pots dry out quickly, while the soil in plastic pots remains moist for a much longer period. On the whole, plastic containers can be recommended and will require only about a third of the amount of water needed for clay ones. Whatever their reputation, cacti do not thrive on neglect; they may survive, but not for long, and eventually you will be left with no plant at all.

CACTI IN THE HOME

Cacti of all kinds make excellent house plants and usually prove easy to grow in the home. The majority of desert types, especially those of compact growth, adapt well to indoor conditions and among them are many species which flower readily and have attractive spines. These are the most suitable for creating a bowl garden and, if carefully planted, they can be a pleasure for years. The main essential is thorough preparation of the container. Choose a bowl which is at least 4 in. (10 cm) deep – the deeper the better – and, to overcome the lack of drainage holes, crock the base well, using broken pieces of clay or pot or medium-sized washed gravel, to a depth of about 1 to $1\frac{1}{2}$ in. (2–3 cm) or more in deeper containers. Then fill up with compost (see p. 23). Charcoal chippings can be included with the crocking to help maintain the sweetness of the compost.

The cacti are best planted in slightly moist compost and left to settle and establish for a week or two in a light airy position. Then firm around the plants and water very carefully. The crocking will act as a reservoir, but it must not be allowed to turn into a pond, for excess water will rot the roots and cause irreparable damage. A hydrometer – a small instrument with a prong which is inserted into the soil down to the base of the container and registers the moisture content – is recommended for these conditions. A rest period is equally important in the home as in the greenhouse, although if the room is kept at a very high temperature occasional moderate watering may be required during dormancy. Fertilizer is also necessary, as the soil is less likely to be changed in a bowl garden than when plants are in pots. Regular feeding during the growing season, about every 10 to 14 days and only in small quantities, will be sufficient.

Among the epiphytic cacti, some of the finest house plants are the *Epiphyllum* hybrids, also termed epicactus. They have been used in this capacity for well over a century, although in those far-off days only a few reds like the hybrid 'Ackermannii' were available which, being readily propagated by cuttings, was a popular plant for the cottage window. Today the hybrids run into hundreds, in every colour except green and blue, from purest white to deepest purple and multicoloured. Almost all are ideally suited for home culture. They are less harmed by overwatering than many other cacti and, with just a little care, will thrive for years.

Other popular cacti with a particularly seasonal appeal are the species and cultivars of *Schlumbergera*, including those previously placed under *Zygocactus*. The typical Christmas cactus with its bright magenta flowers is an old hybrid now known as *Schlumbergera × buckleyi*. In more recent years many new cultivars have found their way into homes throughout Europe and the USA, with flowers of white, pink, pale and deep orange, lilac, deep magenta and even bright yellow. All have what are termed zygomorphic flowers, in which the flower has only one plane of symmetry, and bloom from late November to well into the new year.

The various Easter cacti (formerly under *Rhipsalidopsis*) make very adaptable house plants, flowering profusely in spring to provide an array of colour. The species *Hatiora rosea* and *H. gaertneri* have regular symmetrical flowers of pink and brilliant scarlet respectively, but their hybrids and forms, such as the deep lilac 'Elektra', are very often seen. Although these epiphytic plants have a period of dormancy, in nature they enjoy conditions of uniform moisture and there is no need to dry the soil completely at any time. However, the plants must not become waterlogged and should just be kept slightly moist and fertilized regularly throughout the growing and flowering season.

Once the flower buds have formed on Christmas and Easter cacti, it is important to keep the plant in the same position and not to turn it round, otherwise the buds will be forced to seek light from a different angle and may drop off.

CACTI IN THE GARDEN

The majority of cacti have to be overwintered in frost-free conditions, in the home or greenhouse, but it is a fallacy to suppose that all require protection in winter. In their native habitat many cacti endure the privations of winter and may survive several degrees of frost. However, the soil in which they grow is relatively dry. It is the combination of cold and wet characteristic of northern climes that is the principal reason why more cacti cannot tolerate outdoor culture. Some of the most reliable cacti for growing in the open garden are the *Opuntia* species, especially those from North America where temperatures are comparable to what we are accustomed to in Europe. Species of *Maihuenia*, from high mountainous country in Patagonia, Argentina, and parts of Chile, will also succeed outside. Intense cold is no obstacle to growing such plants, but they should always have a position in maximum light, and, if possible, some sort of shelter from the rain.

The best method is to construct a rockery bed on a slope, which will provide free drainage, and to fill it with very open porous soil – for instance, 1 part loam, 2 parts moss peat or coir and 1 part sharp gritty sand. The inclusion of decayed manure or decomposed leaf-mould will give adequate nourishment to the plants. Choose a sunny south-facing wall as the site, preferably with an overhang or protruding roof to protect the cacti from undue rain and frost.

Propagation

The propagation of cacti is not difficult and there are several methods by which plants can be increased at relatively little cost.

SEED

The advantages of raising cacti from seed are threefold: first, it is economical; secondly, seedlings usually develop true to type and should make good specimen plants; and thirdly, plants adapt themselves to the conditions in which they are to be grown from the beginning of their life. It can also be very rewarding to own spectacular plants which you have raised yourself.

Seeds are fairly easy to obtain. Many excellent seed firms offer mixtures, which are useful for the beginner, although the packets often contain seeds of different sizes according to the various species included. Seeds of numerous species of cacti are also available from specialist nurserymen at moderate prices – affording the satisfaction of knowing precisely what you are sowing, how to deal with and what to expect eventually.

To prepare for sowing, take a small seed tray or pot and cover the base with very gravelly sterilized soil, which will ensure good drainage. Then fill the container with seed compost to within about $\frac{1}{2}$ in. (1.5 cm) of the top, firming well to make a level surface and prevent any puddles when watering. Seeds vary tremendously in size, from a fraction of an inch in diameter to almost dust-like, which is where mixed seed packets can be a problem. They should be spread evenly over the surface of the compost and covered lightly to about their own depth, or left uncovered if very fine.

With only rare exceptions, seed is viable for two years or more, but fresh seed will produce better results. Many species will germinate in a matter of days, while others may take months. After sowing the seeds, stand the container in tepid water without submerging it until the whole surface is thoroughly moistened. Take it out, allow to drain for a while, then cover with glass or paper or both and put in a warm place, preferably a propagating case, out of direct sunlight. A temperature of about 70°F (22°C) should be maintained throughout the germination period. Never allow the compost to dry out, but avoid excessive wet which can rot the seeds and seedlings. Humidity in moderation is helpful, but if

27

excessive moisture condenses on the glass it is too high; in this case, the condensation should be wiped off and the glass kept slightly open to improve ventilation. When germination has taken place, the seedlings should be gradually acclimatized by giving them more and more light and air as they develop.

Seed is best sown early in the year, so long as a regular temperature can be maintained, and the seedlings should be kept growing for at least nine months, preferably through the following winter and into the next normal growing period. The one great danger to seedlings in the early weeks is damping-off, a fungus disease. This can be prevented with a suitable fungicide lightly sprayed over the seedlings the first time they are watered following germination.

Don't be too eager to prick out the seedlings. Wait until they are large enough to handle easily and have acquired some resemblance to the mature plant before planting at a wider spacing. Over-crowding is not necessarily harmful and they can be left un-disturbed for quite a long while, in some cases up to two years.

CUTTINGS AND OFFSETS

Many species can be propagated by cuttings, either by severing the stem sections, or by removing pads (in the case of *Opuntia*) or offsets (as with species of *Echinopsis*, *Mammillaria* and similar plants). This is the quickest method of increasing cacti and it is basically a fairly easy process, but nevertheless requires thought and care. A clean sharp knife should be used to make the cuts and the cuttings should be allowed to dry thoroughly, by exposing the cut surface to the air for several days. They should then be placed firmly in slightly moist, very gritty soil and left in a warm shady position until rooting has taken place. Cuttings should only be taken in warm settled weather and will not require much watering, although occasional spraying overhead helps to stop dehydration.

Species of *Epiphyllum* and kindred genera require slightly different treatment. The stems of *Epiphyllum* can be cut into a number of pieces, each capable of producing a plant. The cuts should be clean and deliberate, from an areole on one side to an areole on the other. Similarly, single or multiple sections can be removed from *Schlumbergera* for propagation. In all cases make sure the cuts have dried thoroughly before potting. A somewhat higher humidity than for desert cacti may speed rooting and the compost can be kept a little moister. A temperature of 70°F (22°C) will encourage rapid root growth and new stem growth will take place in only a matter of weeks. Offsets, which are removed with the roots already developed, are simply potted and grown on as normal plants.

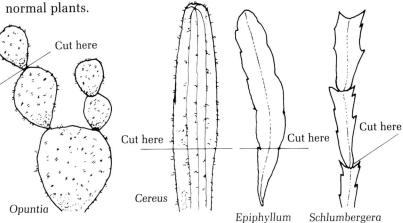

Where to cut when propagating from cuttings

GRAFTING

Grafting is a less common method of propagation, used mainly for species which are inclined to be temperamental or slow growing on their own roots. It consists of joining a stem cutting, called the scion, to the stem of another plant, called the stock. This operation is done without drying either cut, the principles being literally to fuse the two together. The best time to graft is early summer when active growth is apparent, which helps the union.

The most usual and easy procedure, known as the flat graft, is to cut straight across both scion and stock, making sure that the cut surfaces are as equal as possible in area and bevelling or trimming the edges to a slant to prevent the scion falling off as they dry out. The two are then held securely in place with a rubber band until they have united. An alternative is the cleft graft, which is generally used for plants with slender or flat stems like the Christmas cactus. A V-shaped incision is made in the stock and the scion is cut to a wedge shape and fitted into the stock. They can be held together by soft, flexible, thin string or by very carefully placed rubber bands, or a cactus spine can be inserted right through from side to side.

It is important to select the finest stock for grafting. Most globular species take readily to *Echinopsis* stock while many miniature cacti, such as *Blossfeldia*, a very slow-growing species, can be united to *Pereskia* or *Pereskiopsis* stock. *Schlumbergera* and certain epiphytic species of a slow-growing or demanding nature

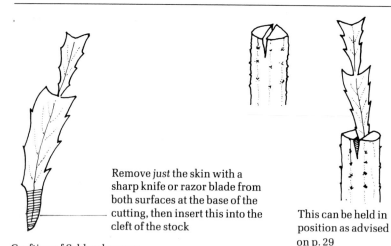

Remove *just* the skin with a sharp knife or razor blade from both surfaces at the base of the cutting, then insert this into the cleft of the stock

This can be held in position as advised on p. 29

Grafting of *Schlumbergera*

can often be grafted to *Selenicereus* or *Pereskia*. The skin only of the scion, which is very narrow, should be carefully removed and immediately inserted into the cleft and held in position as suggested above.

Grafting has a further use with cacti, which is to perpetuate chlorophyll-free forms and cristate or monstrose forms. The absence of chlorophyll, which produces the green colouring in a plant, can lead to many peculiarities. Small seedlings with red, yellow or white plant bodies germinate and feed on the seed leaves and would normally die with them. However, the little seedlings can be saved and, by grafting them to the species of *Trichocereus* or *Hylocereus*, they are able to grow more or less to maturity. The red and yellow knobs offered for sale are the result of this culture, which was developed in Japan.

Cristate (crested) or monstrose forms are abnormal growths which occur in some genera, usually linked with genetic disturbances in the plants. With cristates a fan-shaped growth develops and often becomes wavy and twisted, while monstrose growths are produced by the continued multiplication of the growing points, these being a mass of many miniature shoots. The growths can occur from seedling stage and at any period of the plant's life, but it is possible for them to revert to normal and indeed probable if they are left growing on their own roots. To maintain their attraction, the cristate or monstrose sections are therefore grafted on to suitable stock. The same methods of grafting as for normal forms may be followed, taking care to select large enough stock since both cristates and monstrose forms can grow to an impressive size.

Pests and Diseases

No cacti are immune from pests, but precautions can be taken to minimize their ill-effects. Diseases and disorders, on the other hand, are often due to negligence such as overwatering or bruising and may cause immeasurable harm to the plant body and perhaps even more to the root system.

Some cacti are sensitive to insecticides, but the risk of spray damage can be reduced by applying the insecticide in cool cloudy weather and not when the roots are dry. Remember that chemical insecticides and fungicides are potentially toxic. They should always be handled carefully, given the correct dosages and, above all, stored out of reach of children and pets.

PESTS

Mealybug has the appearance of a soft-bodied, whitish woodlouse, up to $\frac{1}{6}$ in. (4 mm) long, and covered with a white woolly substance. The eggs are contained within the white tufts, which are usually close to the bug. Mild infestations can be dealt with by painting the infested parts with an insecticidal soap. Alternatively, use malathion diluted as prescribed on the bottle, or a systemic insecticide, or in the summer introduce a predatory ladybird, *Cryptolaemus montrouzieri*.

Root mealybugs are smaller and suck sap from the roots and heavy infestations cause poor growth. Examination of the roots should reveal the pests, often surrounded by white waxy powder, on the roots and soil particles. The soil can be gently washed from the roots, which are then dipped in spray-strength malathion before repotting in fresh soil. Systemic insecticides watered on the soil will also help to control attacks.

Red spider mites are yellowish black or reddish orange in colour and minute in size, almost like dust. They become surrounded by very fine webs and suck the sap so that the plant body gradually becomes brownish and disfigured. The cause is generally too dry an atmosphere or bad ventilation and their presence will at least be discouraged if more humidity and air can be introduced. Bifenthrin or malathion can also be used, but a better treatment during the summer is to introduce the predatory mite *Phytoseiulus persimilis*.

Whitefly is an infrequent pest of cacti but may infest the leafy growth of some types. Chemical control is difficult due to the widespread occurrence of resistant strains of the pest. During the summer the parasitic wasp, *Encarsia formosa*, can be introduced and is very effective. At other times, use an insecticidal soap spray.

Scale insects are tiny sap-feeding pests with a shell-like covering on their bodies, rather like a limpet, brown or greyish brown. Eggs are laid under the scale and these hatch into larvae which crawl about looking for a suitable feeding place, when they become immobile for the rest of their lives. Sprays containing malathion or a systemic insecticide are effective, especially if applied when the scales are hatching.

Sciarid fly is most frequently associated with peat-based composts or soils containing a high proportion of undecomposed humus. The $\frac{1}{6}$ in. (3–4 mm) long grey flies lay their eggs in the soil and the small white grubs eat the roots of seedlings and bore into cuttings. They may be controlled by watering the plants with spray-strength malathion.

Many other pests, such as slugs and snails (control by methiocarb or metaldehyde slug pellets), ants and woodlice (control by HCH dust) can attack cacti at times.

DISEASES

Black rot is a common disease which primarily attacks epiphytic cacti. It has been suggested that the complaint is associated with too high a nitrogen content in the soil. The blackening of the stem is usually at soil level or just below and is supposedly caused by the bacteria entering the plant body and turning the tissues black and soft. The diseased area can be cut out, but the operation must be done very thoroughly or the trouble will recur.

Rusty brown spots are not a disease but are mainly due to the retention of water on the exposed body of the plant. Indeed, it should be borne in mind that many troubles can be avoided simply by being observant. When a plant ceases to grow and shows signs of shrivelling, the cause may be over- or under-watering, a need for repotting, or souring of the soil, in which case algae or greenish moss often appear on the surface. Try to prevent problems of your own making or carelessness and you will be rewarded with attractive healthy plants.

Above left: *Rebutia minuscula* f. *kesselringiana*, easily grown and very rewarding (see p.65)
Right: *Gymnocalycium baldianum* may be raised from seed and will flower when 2–3 years old (see p.56)
Below left: *Mammillaria zeilmanniana* can be propagated from offsets (see p.59)
Right: A cristate form of *Parodia leninghausii* (see p.64)

Directory of Cacti

This chapter by no means encompasses the several thousand species of cactus available, nor does it cover all the genera. It is intended, however, as a representative selection of the plants offered by specialist nurseries and garden centres, and is designed to guide the ordinary gardener and also, it is hoped, to meet the aspirations of the enterprising collector and even the connoisseur. The attractive characteristics of the plant, such as shape and flower colour, are described and any special requirements mentioned, together with its suitability for the greenhouse or the home. The entries are divided into two sections – epiphytic cacti (below); and desert cacti (p. 43).

The majority of cacti present little difficulty in cultivation, although some are less easy to obtain than others. Many genera contain species which are suitable for the beginner and not outlandishly expensive and these are widely available from good garden centres, as well as from specialist nurseries. Among them are *Stenocereus*, *Oreocereus* and *Pachycereus* for taller plants and *Echinocactus* and *Ferocactus* for medium to large globular specimens. *Mammillaria* is a magnificent group in its own right with a wealth of different species, ranging from the few with single heads to the many more cushion-forming plants and all flowering readily. Excellent flowering plants are also found within *Notocactus*, *Parodia* and, of course, *Echinopsis*, which has been a popular choice for many years. The numerous species of *Opuntia* are common in garden centres and nurseries, although they should be carefully chosen as some will soon outgrow their allotted space. The Christmas cactus, *Schlumbergera*, and its many hybrids and varieties are old favourites, all very free-flowering and superb house plants. The same applies to *Epiphyllum*, the orchid cactus, which produces truly exotic large flowers from late spring through to early summer.

It may be generally assumed that the cacti offered in garden centres are relatively easy to grow. Rarer, although not necessarily more difficult cacti, can be supplied by specialist nurseries.

EPIPHYTIC CACTI

The epiphytic cacti are a fascinating group of plants whose natural habitat lies mainly in the jungles and rain forests of Central and South America and also the West Indies, where they grow on the trunks and branches of trees or sometimes on rocks. They include some of the most useful house plants, among them the familiar Christmas and Easter cacti. The nomenclature of several species and genera remains confused, but as far as possible the current names are given.

Acanthorhipsalis see *Lepismium*
Aporocactus (Mexico)
Trailing plants with long slender stems, often reaching $3\frac{1}{4}$ ft (1 m). Mostly true epiphytes, even developing aerial roots.
A. flagelliformis, the popular rat's-tail cactus, has stems with 10 to 12 shallow ribs, soft bristly spines and bright crimson zygomorphic (irregular) flowers which last several days. Filtered light rather than full sun is advisable. An acid soil is recommended.
A. flagriformis has long stems with 7 to 10 ribs covered with yellowish spines which often turn brownish. Flowers are deep crimson with a pink suffusion along the margins of the petals, each flower 3 in. (8–9 cm) long.
× *A. mallisonii* is a well known plant with thick pendent stems, well spined, and deep scarlet flowers (see p. 36).
A. martianus has bluish green pendent stems with about 8 low ribs and yellowish spines. Flowers are more or less symmetrical, about $3\frac{1}{2}$ in. (10 cm) long, scarlet-pink, finely lined with violet along the margins. Quite a rare plant, but very free-flowering.
× **Aporophyllum**
Hybrids between *Aporocactus* and *Epiphyllum* and *Disocactus*. Of the many colourful and easily grown cultivars produced, the following are exceptional: 'Cascade' has large shell-pink flowers, the stems long and angled. 'Vivide' is one of the largest, with deep-red flowers and is of Belgian origin. 'Nadine' has 6 to 7 ribbed stems and pinkish purple flowers. 'Najla' carries large bright orange or reddish orange flowers in profusion.
Chiapasia see *Disocactus*
Cryptocereus see *Selenicereus*, *Weberocereus*
Deamia see *Selenicereus*
Disocactus (Central America)
In recent years a considerably enlarged genus as a result of the inclusion of *Pseudorhipsalis*, *Chiapasia* and *Nopalxochia*. Plants with leaf-like, flattened, almost strap-like stems and flowers varying from white to scarlet. Most species are winter-flowering in Europe, so care must be taken to provide sufficient warmth. Useful for hanging baskets and requiring a really rich acid compost.
D. biformis from Guatemala and Honduras has long, serrated, fleshy branches and long slender magenta flowers with a purple style.
D. macrantha (*Pseudorhipsalis macrantha*) has stems with toothed margins, often to nearly $3\frac{1}{4}$ ft (1 m) long. Flowers are fragrant, day-flowering, and appear early in the year – yellowish cream, trumpet-shaped, about $1\frac{1}{2}$ in. (5 cm) long, 1 in. (3 cm) across. Native of Chiapas, Mexico.
D. nelsonii (*Chiapasia nelsonii*) from the forests of south Mexico, and its variety *hondurensis* from Honduras, have many pendent branches, flat and strap-like, the variety more robust than the type. Flowers with a bare, naked tube, trumpet-shaped, 3 in. (8 cm) long and 1 in. (3–4 cm) across, slightly scented but shortlived. Needs very warm and humid conditions to grow successfully.

Above: × *Aporocactus mallisonii*, a well known trailing plant which is excellent for beginners (see p.35)
Below: *Disocactus phyllanthoides* flowers readily and is an ideal house plant (see p.38)

Above: 'Little Sister', one of the delightful *Epiphyllum* hybrids or orchid cacti (see p.38)
Below: *Hatiora gaertneri*, the familiar Easter cactus, a native of Brazil (see p.38)

D. phyllanthoides (*Nopalxochia phyllanthoides*) has thin, flattened stems with notched edges. Flowers are a delicate pink, appearing in early spring, and long-lasting (see p. 36). The cultivar 'Deutsche Kaiserin' is more robust in growth and with larger deep pink flowers.

Epiphyllopsis see *Hatiora*

Epiphyllum (Central and South America, West Indies)
All species have long flattened stems, some shallowly or deeply toothed along the margins. They are of fairly easy culture, preferring an acid soil and temperature of 55°F (12°C). Flowers are white, creamy white or faintly yellow.
E. anguliger from south Mexico has deeply toothed margins along the flat branches and fragrant flowers which bloom by day, all white including the stamens and style.
E. crenatum from Honduras and Guatemala has thick glaucous branches and large scented white flowers, opening by day and long-lasting. This species has been much used in hybridizing with species of *Heliocereus*, *Nopalxochia* and other genera to produce the exotic orchid cacti which make such excellent house plants.

The following are a few of the outstanding cultivars and many more are offered by specialist nurseries: 'Wrayii', a large white with fragrant flowers. 'Celestine', lilac-pink and rose centre. 'Prince Charming', deep rich carmine-red. 'Giant Empress', a large form of 'Deutsche Kaiserin', shades of pink. 'Soraya', a beautiful rich crimson. 'Calypso', a large flower, lilac-pink throughout. 'Pegasus', red to purple shades. 'Celeste', a large flower of pale to deep pink. 'Marseillaise', a rich purplish red. 'Queen Anne', a dwarf plant, good creamy yellow. 'Little Sister', a dwarf with bright salmon-pink flowers (see p. 37). 'Impello', three shades of pink, pale to deep. 'Communion', lilac-pink outer petals, white centre. 'Polar Bear', free-flowering large white. These hybrids are now referred to as epicacti.
E. oxypetalum is widespread from South Mexico to Brazil, with thin, long, often wavy-edged branches developing from tall cylindrical stems, often to 6½ ft (2 m) long. Flowers are borne from the marginal areoles; these are creamy white and have a long curved tube to 1 ft (30 cm) long, hence the name Dutchman's pipe.
E. pumilum from Guatemala is a smaller growing plant with slender flat branches to 1¼ ft (40 cm) long, of pendent habit and best grown in a hanging basket. Flowers are pure white, small, only about 2 in. (5 cm) across, with a protruding white style and sweetly scented.

Erythrorhipsalis see *Rhipsalis*

Hatiora (South America)
A small genus of interesting epiphytes with club-shaped joints or segments, rounded or flat, about ½ in. (1 cm) long, one segment developing from another. Flowers are small, from the tips of the segments, yellow, orange or pink. Plants are spineless and form small bushes. The genus *Pseudozygocactus* is currently considered synonymous.
H. bambusioides has club-shaped joints and orange flowers. The shape of the joint is the main difference from *H. salicornioides*.
H. epiphylloides (*Pseudozygocactus epiphylloides*) has segments arranged similarly to those of *Rhipsalidopsis*, with tiny areoles on the margins of the flat fleshy joints. From the uppermost joints appear small yellowish flowers about ½ in. (1 cm) long. The variety *bradei* differs in the shape of the segments, which are flat, shorter, narrow at the base and widening upwards to form almost a slender triangular joint. This is ideally grown as a grafted plant on *Selenicereus*.
H. gaertneri (*Rhipsalidopsis* (*Schlumbergera*) *gaertneri*), the Easter cactus, has more or less oval stem segments and small areoles with few bristly hairs. Flowers bright scarlet, 1½ in. (4–5 cm) long, from the tips of the segments (see p. 37).
H. herminiae has cylindrical segments in whorls, each segment hardly exceeding ½ in. (1 cm) long. Flowers are deep pink, the petals widely spreading, about 1 in. (2 cm) wide. This is a comparatively new discovery and still rare in cultivation.

H. rosea (*Rhipsalidopsis rosea*) from south Brazil has a rather shrubby habit, often slightly pendent. The smaller stem segments are dark green or slightly reddish with few bristly hairs. Flowers appear from the upper joints in late spring, rose pink in colour, to 1½ in. (4 cm) wide.

H. salicorniodes, called drunkard's dream because of the small bottle-shaped segments, is a forest plant, epiphytic on trees. Flowers are yellowish orange, about ½ in. (1 cm) long, from the terminal ends of the joints. Of easy culture and floriferous.

Hylocereus (Central and South America, West Indies)
Clambering, climbing or semi-pendent robust plants with distinctly angled stems and branches. They are forest plants (*hylos* is a Greek word meaning forest) and develop aerial roots with which to cling to the trees. Most are easy to grow, but can become demanding of space. Flowers are mostly nocturnal, usually large, scented and white or cream, rarely red.

H. calcaratus from Costa Rica and neighbouring countries has fresh green stems with prominent marginal lobes and scarcely spined. Flowers creamy white with bright orange stamens. This will not accept low temperatures.

H. undatus has a wide distribution in nature, but probably originated in the West Indies. It is the commonest member of the genus, with 3-angled stems of deep green, growing to 13 ft (4 m) or more in height. The flowers are large, funnel-shaped, to 1 ft (30 cm) long, creamy white and scented.

Lepismium (South America)
Closely related to *Rhipsalis*, differing principally in the flowers having a sunken ovary. They require an acid soil and humidity.

L. cruciforme from Brazil and Argentina has 3 to 5-angled stems, purplish green or red in colour. Flowers white, followed by reddish purple fruits. The variety *myosurus* has more slender stems with pink flowers.

L. gracilis (*Pfeiffera gracilis*) from Bolivia is a creeping, trailing species with stems up to 2 ft (60 cm) long, slender with 5 to 7 ribs. Numerous tiny, yellowish brown, needle-like spines. Flowers whitish, followed by small, rounded, reddish fruits.

L. houlletiana (*Rhipsalis houlletiana*) from south Brazil has flat leaf-like stems of fresh green with pronounced notches along the margins. Flowers large, to 1 in. (2 cm) long, bell-shaped, creamy white.

L. ianthothele (*Pfeiffera ianthothele*) from Bolivia and Argentina has bright green elongated stems with 3 to 5 ribs and bristly yellowish spines. Flowers are yellowish cream from small areoles appearing along the semi-pendent stem margins. Fruits are a distinctive purplish pink, resembling a miniature gooseberry.

L. micrantha (*Lymanbensonia micrantha*) is a questionable epiphyte, associated with barren areas where it grows on rocks. It is a shrubby plant with long 2 to 3-angled stems, the areoles with spines. Flowers are tubular funnel-shaped, about 1 in. (2–3 cm) long, purplish red. It is generally best grown as an epiphyte, in fairly acid soil in a hanging basket.

L. paradoxum, better known as *Rhipsalis paradoxa*, is a unique species with link-like stem growth, developing in whorls. Flowers and fruits are white.

Lymanbensonia see *Lepismium*
Mediocactus see *Selenicereus*
Nopalxochia see *Disocactus*
Pfeiffera see *Lepismium*
Pseudonopalxochia see *Disocactus*
Pseudorhipsalis see *Disocactus*
Pseudozygocactus see *Hatiora*
Rhipsalidopsis see *Hatiora*
Rhipsalis (South America, West Indies, Madagascar)
Perhaps the most difficult genus of the Cactaceae to understand, as it comprises so many forms and peculiarities and even different characteristics within the same

species. The majority have no spines, but a few have small soft bristles. Flowers are small, regular in shape. Fruits are in the form of small berries. Of easy culture in a semi-shaded position and always kept moist. Suitable for hanging baskets.

R. baccifera (R. fasciculata) from Brazil and Madagascar has cylindrical trailing stems which branch freely, covered by numerous fine, bristly, white hairs. Flowers borne in profusion along the branches, white with pink stamens, and whitish fruits covered with areoles (see p. 12).

R. capilliformis from South Brazil is representative of those with long, pendent, almost thread-like stems to 2 ft (60 cm) or more long. Flowers are white and numerous.

R. cereuscula, a well known species from Brazil and Uruguay, has long slender spines and clusters of small branches in whorls. Flowers white to creamy pink.

R. micrantha (R. tonduzii) from Costa Rica has 3 to 5-angled stems and branches becoming elongated and bushy. Areoles closely set, flowers small, followed by white fruits.

R. pilocarpa (Erythrorhipsalis pilocarpa) has stems rounded, slender and branched, at first erect, becoming pendent, and dark grey to purplish branches in whorls at the terminal ends. Areoles are well distributed, bearing many small bristles. Flowers are carried at the ends of the stems, pinkish cream, slightly scented, to 1 in. (2–3 cm) wide, appearing around Christmas.

R. rhombea from south Brazil closely resembles the Christmas cactus in its stems, which are made up of flat angled joints, dark green, notched and with slightly wavy edges. A pendent plant with creamy white flowers and red fruits.

Schlumbergera (Brazil)
Plants with small leaf-like segments, flat, notched or toothed on the upper part. They have zygomorphic flowers from late autumn to spring, depending on the species. The genus includes the Christmas cactus (previously Zygocactus truncata) and Epiphyllanthus.

S. x buckleyi see under S. truncata.

S. obtusangula (Epiphyllanthus microsphaericus) has jointed stems and rounded ribs, the areoles with many spines and bristles. Flowers purple and rose-pink, opening at the tips to about 2 in. (5 cm) long and fragrant.

S. rondonianus (Arthrocereus rondonianus) is tall-growing to over 1¼ ft (40 cm), the stem bright green with rounded ribs and brownish areoles bearing 50 or more fine golden spines. Flowers a glorious lilac-pink to about 4 in. (10 cm) long.

S. truncata has segments with 2 to 4 teeth on either side near the tips and areoles with few, if any, fine bristly hairs. Flowers pink to violet-red, to 3 in. (8 cm) long, with white filaments and purple style (see p. 21). There is a most attractive white-flowering variety, S. truncata delicatus. The best known of the Christmas cacti, S. x buckleyi (S. bridgesii), has notched segments and flowers of cherry-red (see p. 41). Other hybrids include 'Wintermärchen' (white), 'Pink Beauty' (pink), 'Weihnachts-freude' (orange), 'Lilofee' (pale magenta with paler central stripe), 'Noris' (rich magenta and red-orange), and 'Gold Charm' (the first yellow variant produced).

Selenicereus (Central and South America, West Indies)
Climbing, clambering plants, mostly epiphytic. Good for greenhouse culture, needing space to climb and trail and a large root area. Acid compost is advisable and it must be porous. Flowers diurnal or nocturnal. The genus now includes Deamia, Mediocactus and Strophocactus.

S. anthonyanus (Cryptocereus anthonyanus) from the Chiapas in southern Mexico has long, pendent, flattened stems which develop many aerial roots. Flowers are outstanding and exotic – brick-red sepals, creamy white internally and a bright yellow throat. A desirable species of easy culture. Ideal for hanging baskets.

S. chrysocardium (Epiphyllum chrysocardium, Marniera chrysocardium) known as Heart of Gold, comes from Chiapas in south Mexico and is the largest species in the

Above: *Selenicereus wercklei*, despite its exotic flowers, is not difficult to grow (see p.42)
Below: The Christmas cactus, *Schlumbergera × buckleyi*, is deservedly popular as a house plant (see p.40)

genus. Stems are very wide and deeply serrated, with huge pure white flowers over 1 ft (30 cm) across with pronounced golden filaments. It remains a rarity in collections, but is not difficult to grow.

S. grandiflorus, known as Queen of the Night, originates from Jamaica, Cuba and other West Indian islands. Stems dark green, 5 to 8-ribbed with small brownish spines. Flowers large, white, scented, often to 8 in. (22 cm) long. Rooted cuttings of suitable length make excellent grafting stock.

S. innesii from St Vincent, West Indies, has long spiny stems and branches, in many ways more similar to those of *Aporocactus*. Plants usually produce either male or female flowers, which are white, about 2 in. (5 cm) across, somewhat funnel-shaped, and borne in profusion.

S. megalanthus (*Mediocactus megalanthus*) is native of Peru and Bolivia. Stems are 3-angled, with undulating margins and brownish spines, forming rather dense growth which tends to be more pendent than climbing. The flowers are among the largest of the Cactaceae, to over 1 ft (30 cm) long, white, scented and night-flowering.

S. pteranthus, a Mexican species, has elongated bluish green stems with 4 to 5 ribs, woolly areoles and very short greyish spines. Flowers creamy white, tinged reddish on the outer surfaces. A free-flowering plant of easy culture.

S. testudo, better known as *Deamia testudo*, has 3 to 8 ribs or wings, to about 8 in. (20 cm) long, with aerial roots. Flowers are white or creamy white, to 11 in. (28 cm) long and 8 in. (20 cm) wide, nocturnal. Distributed from southern Mexico to Colombia. The peculiar humped shape of the stems as they climb explains both the botanical name and the common name tortoise cactus.

S. wercklei looks very much like a *Rhipsalis*, slender-stemmed with scarcely any spines or bristles and has white flowers about 6 in. (15 cm) across (see p. 41).

S. wittii (*Strophocactus wittii*), is one of the most extraordinary of all cacti. Sometimes called the strap cactus, it has flattened stems with almost continuous aerial roots from the midrib of the stems and branches, which enable it to climb, together with areoles running along either edge with numerous spines. Flowers are white, night-flowering, to about 10 in. (25 cm) long, with an elongated tube and often reddish sepals. This may be a link plant between *Epiphyllum* and *Selenicereus*. It comes from swampy jungle regions of the Amazon, where frequent floods occur.

Strophocactus see *Selenicereus*

Weberocereus (Central America)

This includes the genus *Werckleocereus*. Stems are slender, ribbed or angled with numerous aerial roots. Flowers are nocturnal, with the moderately long tube bristly or hairy and the ovary with tubercles and small scales.

W. biolleyi very much resembles a *Rhipsalis* in stem growth, which is slightly angled, with aerial roots enabling the plants to climb and clamber. Flowers are small, rose-pink in colour, 1½ to 2 in. (3–5 cm) long. Native of Costa Rica. A pleasing, easily grown species, ideal for a hanging basket.

W. glaber from Guatemala and Costa Rica has bright green, glaucous, 3-angled stems with pronounced projections along the margins from which appear the areoles. Spines are few and small. Flowers white, about 4 in. (10 cm) long, the tube with brownish spines, appearing from the upper areoles. Fruits brick-red.

W. imitans (*Cryptocereus imitans*) from Costa Rica has similar deeply indented 'rick-rack' stems and large, nocturnal, pure white flowers. Ideal for hanging baskets.

W. tunilla, also from Costa Rica, has 4-angled, slender, greyish green stems, occasionally flattened and 12 stiff spines from each areole. A climbing plant with only few aerial roots. Flowers funnel-shaped, about 2½ in. (7 cm) long, rose or purplish pink.

Werkleocereus see *Weberocereus*

Zygocactus see *Schlumbergera*

DESERT CACTI

The term 'desert' is not entirely accurate. While many cacti experience the arid conditions prevailing in both North and South America, these are not permanent but spasmodic, whether for weeks, months or years. Rain eventually falls and there are often moist mists pervading vast areas or heavy dews. Consequently, the plants which inhabit such regions can obtain sufficient nourishment for their survival and cacti, which have the advantage of internal water-storage facilities, absorb moisture when it becomes available to use in periods of drought.

The very structure of cacti, gradually evolved over the centuries, helps to protect them from excess evaporation. The fleshy stems which serve as storage organs are globular or elongated to reduce the surface area and the spines are modified leaves; the rib formation is designed to counteract the intense heat of the sun and remains unchanged in drought or deluge, although the surface between contracts as drought is prolonged and expands as rain falls to take in moisture. Another evolutionary development are the thick succulent pads of opuntias, heavily or thinly covered with areoles, glochids and spines, which constitute the stem and branches of the plants.

In cultivation, correct watering is one of the most important ingredients for success. From late March, give a good soaking when the soil is really dry, waiting until the soil dries out again before repeating the process, and continue until late October or early November. Then keep the plants completely dry throughout the winter and early spring before starting again. This is the general rule for desert cacti, but any peculiarity will be noted in the following list.

Acanthocalycium (Argentina)
A genus of about 2 species of somewhat globular plants with several ribs, many spines and beautifully coloured flowers.
A. *spiniflorum* is the tallest of the genus, to about 2 ft (60 cm) high and 6 in. (15 cm) wide, and an elegant plant with about 20 ribs, very spiny at the crown. Flowers funnel-shaped, rose-pink, woolly on the exterior with yellowish spiny scales.
A. *violaceum* grows to about 8 in. (20 cm) tall and 4 in. (10 cm) wide, with 15 to 18 ribs, yellowish spines and rose-lilac flowers opening to 2 in. (5–6 cm) across.
Arequipa see Oreocereus
Ariocarpus (Mexico and southern USA)
A genus of about 7 species, often likened to living rock on account of the gnarled, almost triangular tubercles encompassing the plant body. Plants have long, fleshy, tapering roots. Full sun, sandy soil with lime added and careful watering are essential.

Above: *Astrophytum asterias* (left) and *A. myriostigma* (right) two examples of this popular and undemanding genus (see p.45)
Below: *Mammillaria elongata* belongs to one of the largest and most important genera of cacti (see p.59)

A. agavoides (*Neogomesia agavoides*) has thick, spreading tubercles resembling the leaves of an agave, with areoles at the tips. A rare plant, about 2½ in. (7 cm) wide. Flowers late in the year, pink, funnel-shaped and to 1½ in. (4 cm) wide.

A. kotschoubeyanus is only about 1 in. (2 cm) across the flattened surface of the plant, which consists of symmetrically arranged, small, triangular tubercles. Flowers pink or pale purple, ¾ in. (2 cm) wide.

A. trigonus is probably the largest in the genus, to 1 ft (30 cm) wide. Tubercles numerous, yellowish green, triangular with flat upper surface and horny. Flowers yellowish.

Arrojadoa (Brazil)
Plants have long, slender, cylindrical stems with a bristly cap or cephalium at the tip from which the flowers appear. New growth continues through the cephalium to form another cephalium for future flowering and the stem is therefore ringed at intervals with thick clusters of bristly hairs.

A. penicillata has long branching stems, often prostrate, 6½ ft (2 m) long, and 10 to 12 low ribs armed with fine spreading spines. Flowers bunched at apex, carmine-pink, about ¾ in. (2 cm) long. A free-flowering species.

A. rhodantha is of clambering habit, with stems to 6½ ft (2 m) long, up to 14 low ribs, dark green, and about 25 slender spines. Flowers about 1 in. (3 cm) long, pink.

Arthrocereus see *Schlumbergera*

Astrophytum (Mexico)
A popular and fascinating genus in which each species has distinctive features, some being spineless. Soil must be porous with lime added. Plants should be kept dry during dormancy and watered moderately throughout the growing season.

A. asterias is a squat globular plant, having almost flat ribs with defined furrows. It is spineless, but the woolly areoles are few and pronounced so the whole body is dotted with white. Flowers yellow, reddish in the centre, 1½ in. (3–4 cm) long and wide (see p. 44).

A. capricorne has long, twisted, blackish brown spines set on broadly spaced ribs. Flowers pale yellow with numerous petals and carmine-red centres.

A. myriostigma, called the bishop's cap, is somewhat rounded in shape, but becomes columnar with age. Generally with only 3 to 5 ribs and covered with whitish scales. Flowers yellow, sometimes reddish in centre (see p. 44). There are several varieties.

A. ornatum is a more columnar plant, at least in maturity. There are a number of forms, mostly with about 8 ribs and few yellowish brown spines, and the body may be coloured green, white, grey or partially mottled. Flowers yellow with red centres (see p. 12).

Austrocactus (South America)
A small genus of 5 species which is still quite rare in cultivation. Small columnar plants having stems densely armed with long spines, often with aerial roots.

A. patagonicus from south Argentina and Chile grows to about 1½ ft (50 cm) and 3 in. (8 cm) wide. It has straight and hooked spines of yellowish brown and white, pinkish flowers with a prominent deep violet stigma, to about 2 in. (5 cm) wide.

Aztekium (Mexico)
A. ritteri, the only species, is somewhat globular and flattened in shape, about 2 in. (5 cm) wide and with a long taproot. It has about 10 ribs and olive-green, closely set, minute areoles with horizontal furrows from areole to areole. Spines few, papery and flattened. The structure of the body suggests an Aztek sculpture – whence the name. Tiny, whitish, funnel-shaped flowers. Offsets are produced from the base. A much sought-after plant.

Backebergia see *Pachycereus*

Blossfeldia (Argentina and Bolivia)
Miniature plants, mostly multi-headed, which are difficult on their own roots and best grafted. The genus contains just 4 species, all rare.

B. liliputana is a flattish cylindrical plant, greyish green with minute, grey, woolly areoles, spineless. Flowers whitish pink from near the apex. From Argentina.
B. minima from Bolivia is the smallest species yet discovered within the Cactaceae, less than ½ in. (1 cm) in diameter. Similar to *B. liliputana* in colouring and flower.

Buiningia see *Coleocephalocereus*

Carnegiea (southern USA and Mexico)
Named in honour of the philanthropist Andrew Carnegie and contains a single species – the famous saguaro so often considered typical of cacti.
C. gigantea is a slow-growing species which can be easily contained in cultivation for very many years, although it ultimately becomes tree-like. Stems dark green to 45 ft (14 m) tall, 2¼ ft (70 cm) thick in the wild. Many blunt ribs with dark brown spines. Flowers open in the evening and last well into the following day; they are white, greenish externally, funnel-shaped, from near the top of the stems. It has edible fruits. Easy to grow, but patience is necessary to develop a large specimen.

Cephalocereus (Mexico)
What was once a large genus now comprises only two species.
C. senilis, the old man cactus, is a very distinctive columnar plant completely covered with long white hairs which envelop the stem from top to base. Flowers rose-pink, about 2 in. (5 cm) long. On mature plants 19 ft (6 m) tall a cephalium is formed. A must for every collector and reasonably easy in cultivation, requiring complete dryness in winter (see pp. 24 and 51).

Cereus (South America, West Indies)
Tall stately plants, often branched. All are nocturnal flowering and invariably fragrant. A large genus of easy culture.
C. chalybaeus grows to about 10 ft (3 m) and occasionally branches. Ribs about 6 with black spines very distinctive against the bluish colouring of the stems. Flowers large, white, pinkish externally. From Argentina and Uruguay.
C. haageanus (*Monvillea haageana*) from Paraguay grows to 10 to 13 ft (3–4 m) high, branching freely, pale blue-green in colour, with a few white brownish-tipped spines and one longer black central. Flowers about 5 in. (12 cm) long, pure white.
C. hildmannianus (*C. peruvianus*) is a branching species to about 10 ft (3 m) or more tall. There is also a very fine monstrose form (see p. 14). Stems are dark green with 9 broad ribs and blackish spines. Flowers 6 in. (15 cm) wide, white. Apparently extinct in the wild. Useful for grafting.
C. spegazzinii (*Monvillea spegazzini*) from Paraguay has bluish green stems, marbled white and grey, 3-angled with large tubercles and black-spined areoles. Flowers pinkish white with a long tube, about 5 in. (13 cm) long. There is also an interesting cristate form available.
C. validus (*C. forbesii*) from Argentina grows to 19 ft (6 m) or more, often branched. Stems are bluish green, later turning to dull green. Ribs about 6 with large yellowish brown areoles and long, awl-shaped, yellowish, later almost black spines. Flowers white, funnel-shaped, to 8 in. (20 cm) long.

Chamaecereus see *Echinopsis*

Cleistocactus (South America)
Columnar plants of erect or clambering habit, often branching from the base. Flowers tubular, the tips barely opening with only the style and stamens protruding. Fruits are small red berries. Of easy culture.
C. icosagonus (*Borzicactus aurivillus*) from north Peru has clustering stems of bright green with notched ribs bearing yellow woolly areoles and numerous translucent fine spines. Flowers red, about 2 in. (5 cm) long.
C. roezlii (*Seticereus borzicactus roezlii*) from north Peru has pale green stems divided into many ribs armed with light brownish yellow spines. Flowers are red, 2 in. (5 cm) long.
C. smaragdiflorus from Argentina and Bolivia is a slender stemmed plant with about 15 ribs and long brownish spines. Flowers are straight, wine-red in colour with a

colourful green pointed tip, in all about 2 in. (4–5 cm) long.

C. strausii from Bolivia is the best known species. Erect bristly stems, the silvery white bristles arising from the closely set, white, woolly areoles. Flowers protrude straight and horizontally from the stem, dark carmine-red, the tube scaly and hairy. One of the most beautiful of cacti.

C. wendlandiorum is probably the most uncommon of the genus. Stout stems of greyish green with golden yellow spines and rich deep orange flowers. Native of west Argentina.

C. winteri (*Borzicactus auriespinus*, *Hildewintera auriespina*) is a lovely species from Bolivia, pendent, spreading, with golden yellow spines. Orangey red flowers freely produced.

Coleocephalocereus (Brazil)
An interesting genus, previously known as *Buiningia*, with mostly cylindrical stems and a dense, woolly, bristly cap (cephalium) which gradually covers nearly all one side of the plant.

C. aureus (*Buiningia aureum*, *B. brevicylindrica*), is inclined to become cylindrical. It offsets freely from the base with heavily spined plantlets. Flowers greenish yellowish white appearing from near the top of the cephalium (see p. 48). It has pronounced areoles, many yellowish spines becoming grey. Golden yellow bristles of the cephalium become blackish with age. Flowers small, yellowish green.

C. purpureus (*Buiningia purpurea*) is a columnar plant to nearly 3¼ ft (1 m) tall, rich green, the areoles having many reddish or yellowish brown spines. A grey woolly cephalium with reddish or yellowish bristles protruding. Flowers reddish purple, about 1 in. (3 cm) long.

Copiapoa (Chile)
The name refers to the Chilean city of Copiapo. Globular plants often forming dense groups, greyish, even quite silvery, which is a distinctive feature. They tolerate cold and are much sought-after.

C. cinerea has a whitish grey body with dense white wool in the crown and pro-truding brownish black bristles. Ribs broad, about 18, with closely set areoles and small black spines. Flowers are yellow, from the crown. The erstwhile *C. haseltoniana* certainly has longer spines, but is considered synonymous.

C. krainziana from Chile is exceptional, with a wide greyish green body to about 4½ in. (12 cm), the areoles having long, white, hair-like bristles and golden spines and the crown grey and woolly. Rather uncommon in cultivation.

Coryphantha (Mexico and USA)
A large genus of globular plants with tubercles bearing stiff spines. Flowers usually in the crown of the plant. Very porous soil is necessary, preferably with lime added. Full sun is essential for good flowering, but only moderate watering in summer.

C. clava is bluish green in colour and can attain 1 ft (30 cm) in height. Tubercles are conical, with yellowish or brownish spines. Flowers large, yellow tipped red.

C. elephantidens has a dark green, glossy body to 6 in. (15 cm) tall and large rounded tubercles, with white wool in the axils. Spines brownish, outward spreading. Flowers in varying shades of pink, often with a brownish sheen, about 4 in. (10 cm) wide.

C. poselgeriana has a bluish green body, eventually to about 8 in. (20 cm) tall, with wide tubercles tipped with areoles bearing reddish brown, almost blackish spines. Flowers are whitish or yellowish with a rose-pinkish throat.

Discocactus (South America)
A genus which contains some of the most unusual species of cacti, many discovered only in recent years. The plant body is globose, often somewhat flattened, and with maturity develops a cephalium from which the nocturnal flowers appear. All species are considered rarities and are not easy to grow.

D. boomianus from Brazil is a heavily spined species, the spines completely covering the greyish green body, which is about 2 in. (5 cm) tall, 3–7 in. (8–20 cm) wide, with

Above left: *Pachycereus militaris*, unmistakeable for its busby-like cap (see p.63)
Right: *Coleocephalocereus aureus*, showing the unusual red seed pod (see p.47)
Below: *Copiapoa cinerea* has the chalky body characteristic of the genus, which is somewhat difficult in cultivation

many bumpy ribs. Flowers are white, rather funnel-shaped, about 3 in. (8 cm) wide. *D. hartmannii* from Paraguay is of similar dimensions, with about 16 ribs, notched into conical tubercles tipped with woolly areoles, and some 12 radial spines. Cephalium without spines or bristles. Flowers to 4 in. (10 cm) long, funnel-shaped, about 2 in. (5 cm) across at the tips. A lovely species which flowers readily. *D. horstii* from south Brazil is one of the miniature species, the body only about 2 in. (5–6 cm) wide, with about 20 ribs, closely set areoles and minute comb-like spines. The cephalium is white and woolly with a few brownish bristles, and the white flowers are to 2 in. (6 cm) long. It can be successfully grown if grafted.

Echinocactus (Mexico and USA)
These are large and beautiful barrel-shaped cacti, mostly heavily spined but with only small flowers. Although numerous species were formerly included in the genus, reclassifications have reduced the number to nine. Sun-loving plants.
E. grusonii from Mexico is known as golden barrel or sometimes as mother-in-law's cushion. It is spectacular throughout its life, often reaching over 3¼ ft (1 m) tall and 2 ft (60 cm) or more wide, having many sharp ribs and long golden yellow spines. Flowers appear from around the crown of the plant, but only after many years, and are small, about 2 in. (5 cm) long and bright yellow. Very easy plants in cultivation with comparatively rapid growth (see p.2 and p.51).
E. horizonthalonius from southern USA and north Mexico grows to about 10 in. (25 cm) high and 1¼ ft (40 cm) wide. Stems globular, greyish green with about 8 broad ribs, deeply furrowed between. Areoles woolly, bearing 6 to 9 flattened, stiff, thick, yellowish brown spines. Flowers pink, about 1 in. (3 cm) long, occasionally longer. Essentially a sun-loving species.
E. platyacanthus (*E. ingens*) can attain 3¼ ft (1 m) or so tall and wide. Plants have about 50 ribs with woolly yellowish areoles and brownish spines. The plant body is greenish grey and very woolly on the crown. Flowers bright yellow, 1 in. (3 cm) long, about 1½ in. (4 cm) wide, reddish externally. It is a native of Mexico and requires a compost which is porous and contains lime.

Echinocereus (Mexico and western USA)
The word *echinos* means hedgehog and the description certainly fits most of the 60-odd species in the genus. Plants are spiny and low-growing and normally have large, colourful, long-lasting flowers, a distinctive feature being the green stigma which is apparent in nearly every species. Some form large clumps and the majority are of easy culture, provided they are kept dry in winter. A few, notably *E. viridiflorus*, may be grown outside.
E. coccineus (*neo-Mexicanus*) from New Mexico and other southern states of the USA, which has large bright yellow flowers to 4 in. (10 cm) long, opening to nearly 5 in. (12 cm) across.
E. engelmannii is rather variable in spination, sometimes with blackish tips, otherwise with brown or yellow. Stems grow to about 8 in. (20 cm) tall, forming clumps. Flowers purple-red.
E. knippelianus, a very distinctive species which does not cluster, is globular to oval in shape, with 5 prominent ribs, woolly areoles and few thin spines. Flowers pale magenta produced freely in spring. A desirable plant.
E. leucanthus (*Wilcoxia albiflora*) is a much-branching plant from Guasima in Sonora, where it grows among low scrub near the waterfront. Stems are slender, soft and clambering, with closely pressed fine spines. White terminal flowers with greenish brown throat are about 1 in. (3 cm) long, ¾ in. (2 cm) across (see p.69).
E. pectinatus from central Mexico grows to 6 to 8 in. (15–20 cm) high and to 2 in. (6 cm) wide, only rarely clustering. Plants have over 20 ribs with elongated areoles and comb-like spines closely pressed to the short cylindrical stem. Flowers are purplish pink, 2 to 3 in. (6–8 cm) long and wide.
E. pentalophus is a low-growing clustering species, stems to 5 in. (12 cm) long, pale

green with about 5 ribs, the areoles bearing a few greyish short spines. A sprawling plant of easy culture, the flowers large, funnel-shaped, pink or lilac with a white throat, 4 in. (10 cm) long and across.

E. poselgeri (*Wilcoxia poselgeri*) has very long, slender, greyish green stems, minute spines and purplish pink flowers, the tube having many small spines and whitish hairs. From Texas and north Mexico.

E. pulchellus is globular in shape, bluish green in colour, and has 12 ribs with small areoles bearing 3 to 4 very short yellow spines. Flowers are white to deep rose, funnel-shaped, to about 1½ in. (4 cm) long.

E. viridiflorus from Dakota and Wyoming is globular, often clustering, dark green in colour with about 12 low ribs and elongated areoles. Both radial and central spines are slender but stiff and coloured white or reddish brown. Flowers are borne freely from the side areoles, each about 1 in. (2–3 cm) long, greenish with a darker midrib. It needs the driest possible place, but accepts full exposure to frost.

Echinofossulocactus see *Stenocactus*

Echinopsis (South America)

The merging of *Trichocereus* and *Lobivia* with *Echinopsis* has increased the number of species now recognized under this name. Most of the original species are well known and easily grown plants which flower freely, although the flower lasts only a day.

E. chamaecereus (*Lobivia silvestrii*) commonly called the peanut cactus, is from high altitudes in Argentina. It makes strong rapid growth with a series of blunt, small, cylindrical stems resembling peanuts in shape. Stems have short bristly spines and bright red flowers are borne in profusion. May be grown outside, kept as dry as possible from October to March (see p. 61).

E. cinnabarina (*Lobivia cinnabarina*) is a solitary plant, only occasionally offsetting, with a long slender tap-root and dark green, waxy, globular stem 4 to 6 in. (10–15 cm) wide, with about 20 spirally arranged, warty ribs and many long curved spines. The funnel-shaped, deep red flowers are about 3 in. (8 cm) wide at the tips. A charming Bolivian species, the flowers lasting for two days.

E. eyriesii is a globular plant, native of south Brazil and Argentina, reaching to 6 in. (15 cm) or more tall and about 5 in. (12 cm) thick. It has many acute ribs and short dark brown spines protruding from round greyish areoles. Large, funnel-shaped, fragrant, white flowers, 6½ to 10 in. (17–25 cm) long and to 5 in. (12 cm) broad, appear in late afternoon and last well into the following morning. There are several forms, varying mostly in flower colour.

E. ferox (*Lobivia backebergii*) from Bolivia has pale green stems with about 15 spirally arranged, acute and notched ribs. There are up to 7 brownish, spreading radial spines, slender and often curved. It rarely clusters. Flowers from upper part of stem, rich carmine in colour, about 1½–2 in. (4–5 cm) long.

E. huasha (*Helianthocereus huasha*) is a low-growing semi-erect species with cylindrical stems, each with about 18 rounded ribs, close-set areoles bearing numerous yellowish brown spines. Flowers are either red or yellow, day-flowering, 2½ to 4 in. (7–10 cm) long. From Argentina.

E. leucantha is an oblong plant with about 15 ribs, curved brownish spines and one long curved spine. Flowers are very large, about 8 in. (20 cm) long, nocturnal and sweetly scented. From northwest Argentina.

E. macrogona (*Trichocereus macrogonus*) from Bolivia and Argentina is an elegant fast-growing species, rather bluish green with about 7 low ribs, and short brownish spines, but longer centrals. Flowers are white, about 7 in. (18 cm) long, and nocturnal.

E. marsoneri (*Lobivia jajoiana*) an outstanding species, is usually solitary with a bright green cylindrical or oval stem and many notched ribs, the sunken areoles bearing about 10 whitish radical spines and one central. Flowers fragrant, funnel-

Above left: The distinctive *Cephalocereus senilis* or old man cactus from Mexico (see p.46)
Right: *Echinocactus grusonii*, which can quickly reach a large size (see p.49), with *Opuntia microdasys* (see p.62)
Below: *Echinocereus scheerii*, a widely available species, has flowers lasting over a week

shaped, about 2 in. (6 cm) long and across, from the sides of the stem, in shades of red
with a bluish suffusion, yellow or orange, always with a blackish throat from which
arise numerous stamens. From north Argentina.

E. oxygona is widespread in south Brazil, Argentina and Uruguay. Stems at first
globular becoming cylindrical to 1 ft (30 cm) tall and about 8 in. (20 cm) diameter.
The body somewhat greyish green and offsetting at ground level. It has even, acute
ribs with large areoles and spreading, awl-shaped, pale brownish spines. Flowers
are white, flushed with pink on the inner surface, deeper reddish externally, about
10 in. (25 cm) long, opening at night. Plants formerly listed as *E. multiplex* are now
classified in this species.

E. thionantha (*Acanthocalycium aurantiacum*), a low-growing species with rounded
stems, to 3½ in. (9 cm) wide and barely 2 in. (5 cm) high, greyish green in colour with
15 or more ribs and many long yellowish spines with black tips. Flowers bright
orange-yellow, 2 in. (5 cm) across.

Many colourful hybrids have been created by crossing *E. eyriesii* and other
species. Mostly flowering by day in shades ranging from yellow and orange to pink
and red, all are of very easy culture.

E. spachiana (*Trichocereus spachianus*) grows to 6½ ft (2 m) high, glossy green with
about 12 to 15 ribs. A spiny plant with about 10 radials and 2 to 3 centrals. Flowers
white, nocturnal, from apex of plant, each about 8 in. (20 cm) long, 6 in. (15 cm)
across. From Argentina.

Encephalocarpus see *Pelecyphora*

Epithelantha (Mexico and south Texas)
An attractive genus of one species and a number of varieties.

E. micromeris is small and compact, either solitary or offsetting from the base to
form clusters, with a neat globular stem about 2 in. (6 cm) high, completely covered
with spirally arranged tubercles bearing tufts of dense, silvery white, slender spines.
Small flowers are produced from the crown, appearing at the tips of the new
tubercles, white or pink with only very few petals. Fruits are club-shaped, bright
red, maturing the following year. Of slow growth, requiring a calcareous soil and a
sunny location.

Eriocereus see *Harrisia*

Escobaria (southern USA and Mexico)
A genus of currently about 12 species which is very close to *Neobesseya*, the difference lying mainly in the fruit and seeds. Globular or semi-cylindrical stems,
generally tufted with very attractive spination.

E. asperispina (*Neobesseya asperispina*) is mostly solitary, dark bluish green to 2 in.
(6 cm) thick, with soft, pointed, conical tubercles, inclined to be flat on the upper
side. Flowers pale greenish yellow, to 1 in. (3 cm) long and wide.

E. chaffeyi from Mexico grows to about 5 in. (12 cm) high, 2 in. (5–6 cm) thick, with
many long, bristly, white radial spines and 1 to 3 shorter blackish-tipped centrals.
Flowers small, yellowish white, the petals with a brown line down the centre.

E. missouriensis from USA is a variable species, with glaucous green, globular stems
to 2 in. (6 cm) high, usually clustering, and very pronounced tubercles grooved on
the upper side. Many needle-like grey spines. Flowers greenish yellow, to 1 in. (3 cm)
long, stamens yellow and green stigma with 2 to 5 lobes.

E. runyonii ranges from the Rio Grande in Texas into Mexico and is a popular plant
of clustering habit. Stems round or oblong, 1½ in. (3–5 cm) long and greyish green,
the tubercles cylindrical, with many white, needle-like, radial spines and thicker,
longer, brownish-tipped central spines. Flowers pale purple, about ½ in. (1.5 cm)
long, with a purple median line on the petals. Stamens purplish, stigma with 6 green
lobes.

Espostoa (Peru and Ecuador)
Very attractive nocturnal-flowering cacti of columnar habit, often with long white

Above: *Pelecyphora strobiliformis*, a most desirable cactus but difficult to grow successfully (see p.64)
Below: *Epithelantha micromeris*, with very dense short spines similar to many *Mammillaria* species

hairs, developing a dense woolly cap with maturity. Require full sun and watering in moderation, but easy to grow. There are 13 species in the genus.

E. lanata from altitudes of over 6,500 ft (2,000 m) is a beautiful species of slow growth, to about 3¼ ft (1 m) high, with rounded ribs, whitish areoles bearing glistening yellow or reddish spines and 1 to 2 longer central spines plus numerous silky white hairs completely covering the plant. Flowers are white, small, developing from the cephalium.

E. melanostele is a more robust species, with darker green stems, more or less hairy, and develops a brownish cephalium with age. The flowers are pinkish white.

Eulychnia (South America)

Columnar plants, often reaching tree-like proportions, many-ribbed and spiny, with small bell-shaped flowers. Easily raised from seed and generally of easy culture.

E. acida is a tall growing plant with 12 rounded ribs, mainly long, spreading radial spines and 1 to 4 long central spines of greyish brown. Flowers 2 in. (5–6 cm) long and wide, with a short woolly tube and pink petals.

E. breviflora (E. saint-pieana) from north Chile grows to about 13 ft (4 m) in its native habitat, but rarely exceeds 3¼ ft (1 m) in cultivation. Radial spines 8 to 12 and a long greyish brown central developing from white woolly areoles. Flowers white, 2 to 3 in. (5–7 cm) long and wide, often with pinkish central lines.

Ferocactus (southern USA, Mexico, Guatemala)

Large barrel-shaped plants with particularly distinctive strong spines, curved, straight or hooked, apparent even when quite young. They present no difficulties in cultivation, needing a sunny position and generous watering during the growing period, but take several years to reach maturity and flower. The genus *Hamatocactus* is now included here.

F. cylindraceus (F. acanthodes) from Mexico and USA is concentrated in Baja California. Tall-growing in the wild, often to 10 ft (3 m) high, but in cultivation usually seen as more globular plants. Stems are glaucous green, 13 to 23 broad ribs, sunken areoles with many distinctive straight or curved red and bright yellow spines, densely arranged. Flowers form near the crown of the plant, yellow or pale orange. Easy to grow, but slow to reach maturity. It should have an open rich compost with some lime and moderate watering, being kept totally dry in winter (see p. 24).

F. emoryi (F. covillei) from the Sonora and Arizona deserts, can reach to over 3¼ ft (1 m) high in some habitats; in others it remains relatively small, even with age, and in this case often develops offsets from the base. Flowers reddish or reddish yellowish.

F. fordii is a smaller-growing species from Baja California, to only about 1½ ft (40 cm) high. A beautiful, interesting plant with pinkish rose flowers formed in a ring around the crown (see p. 55).

F. latispinus from central areas of Mexico, invariably at altitudes of about 9,800 ft (3,000 m), is one of the most popular species. Stem more or less globular, to about 1 ft (30 cm) high, greyish green with up to 20 ribs. Radial spines reddish or white and 4 central deep red spines, the lower one strongly hooked. Flowers whitish or reddish white, about 1½ in. (4 cm) long.

F. viridescens is a globular species to about 1¼ ft (40 cm) high and over 1 ft (35 cm) thick. New spines are red, gradually fading to pink. Flowers greenish yellow and rather small.

Frailea (South America)

A genus of about 22 species, all of relatively small, almost miniature growth. Mostly globular or becoming elongated and grouping. Flowers are pollinated without actually opening. Good light, not necessarily full sun, and a slightly acid compost are necessary.

F. asterioides from north Uruguay and Brazil is a variable species, but generally only

Above left: *Harrisia guelichii* produces its striking large flowers at night (see p.56)
Right: *Espostoa melanostele* looks as if it is enveloped in spun wool (see p.54)
Below: *Ferocactus fordii*, an unusual diminutive species in this normally tall-growing genus (see p.54)

about 1 in. (3 cm) wide, reddish brown in colour, with up to 15 virtually spineless ribs, very much like a small sea urchin. Flowers pale yellow, about 1½ in. (4 cm) across.

F. curvispina is another diminutive species, with many warty ribs and yelllowish, curved, twisted radial spines and one central. Flowers are about 1 in. (3 cm) across, bright yellow. From Brazil.

F. matoana is native of south Brazil, a small globular plant, reddish brown in colour, with rounded tubercles and minute spines. Flowers are brown and yellow.

Gymnocactus see *Turbinocarpus*

Gymnocalycium (South America)
A large genus of some 80 or more species, globular with chin-like tubercles. Plant surface usually smooth and waxy. Flowers small to large, bell-shaped. Not difficult in cultivation so long as the soil is relatively porous and fairly acid. They require careful watering and a position in indirect light is probably better than full sun.

G. baldianum from Argentina has a bluish green body to about 2½ in. (6 cm) wide, 9 to 11 ribs, 5 to 7 radial spines and beautiful deep red flowers to 2 in. (5 cm) long from around the crown (see p. 33).

G. bruchii is a small clustering species, having dark green stems with about 12 ribs. Spines may be long or short, either flat to the body of the plant or projecting, yellowish brown in colour. Flowers are borne in profusion, pale pink. Propagation is easy by rooting of offsets. From Argentina.

G. mihanovitchii has a grey-green body with reddish markings forming transverse bands around the plant and stems up to 2 in. (6 cm) wide with a few fine spines. Flowers are yellowish white or slightly pinkish. There are a number of varieties including *friedrichiae*, with rose-pink flowers. Seeds frequently germinate to produce yellow or red seedlings, which are said to be mutations. These chlorophyll-free forms are the popular red and yellow knobs and can only survive by grafting (see also p. 30).

G. saglionis is one of the largest species in the genus, often to about 1 ft (30 cm) high and wide, bluish green in colour with pronounced chins and red and greyish curved spines. Flowers about 1–2 in. (3–4 cm) long, pinkish white.

Haageocereus (South America)
The genus is named in honour of one of the greatest figures in 'cactology', Walter Haage of Erfurt. Of the 20 species recognized, some are columnar and erect, others prostrate and branching from the base. Most have rich golden spines and beautiful nocturnal flowers borne on a long scaly tube, opening in late afternoon and continuing well into the following morning.

H. decumbens from south Peru has stems to about 3¼ ft (1 m) long, semi-prostrate and clambering, with about 20 ribs and spines yellowish or reddish gradually turning grey. Flowers are sweetly scented, about 2½ in. (7 cm) long, white, brownish externally. Fruits are bright pink and roundish with a few hairy scales.

H. versicolor, from north Peru, reaches over 3¼ ft (1 m) tall and about 2 in. (5 cm) thick, with about 20 ribs, covered with yellowish or reddish spines. The flowers are about 4 in. (10 cm) long, white on the inner surface, greenish outside.

Hamatocactus see *Ferocactus* and *Thelocactus*

Harrisia (South America and West Indies)
This genus of tall, often climbing plants now includes plants formerly classified as *Eriocereus*. Vigorous-growing plants with nocturnal flowers and large red fruits.

H. bonplandii (*Eriocereus bonplandii*) from Brazil, Argentina and Paraguay has stems to 10 ft (3 m) long, 1 to 2 in. (3–6 cm) thick, bluish or greyish green, with 4 to 6 ribs. Areoles with 3 to 5 grey spines. Flowers white, brownish green externally, to 10 in. (25 cm).

H. guelichii (*Eriocereus guelichii*) has long, sprawling, thin stems, pale green in colour with 3 to 4 prominent ribs, 4 to 5 radial and 1 longer central spine to each

Above: One of the *Ferocactus* species from Baja California in flower
Below: *Gymnocalycium denudatum*, a popular member of the genus with
spider-like spines

areole. Flowers large and showy, about 10 in. (25 cm) long, white with long prominent stamens. A fast-growing, free-flowering species requiring a porous soil without lime. From Argentina.

H. martinii (*Eriocereus martinii*) has greenish grey sprawling stems to over 6½ ft (2 m) long, with 4 to 5 wide ribs, areoles with 5 to 7 short spines, straight and stiff. Flowers about 8 in. (20 cm) long, white inner petals, greenish and red-tipped externally. Argentina.

Helianthocereus see *Echinopsis*

Heliocereus (Mexico and Guatemala)
Clambering or semi-erect plants with 3 to 4-angled stems, areoles set well apart, large and felted with stiffish spines. They often have aerial roots, but are not epiphytic. The flowers are magnificent and certain species including *H. speciosus* have been crossed with *Epiphyllum* to produce the numerous orchid cacti (see p. 38). They need an acid soil, a minimum temperature of 45°F (70°C) and a bright position, but not full sun.

H. speciosus is a startlingly attractive and popular species with its brilliant rich scarlet flowers, to about 6 in. (15 cm) long with a green scaly tube. Generally of semi-erect habit, with stems 3 to 4-angled and yellow spines. There are also the varieties *superbus* with thicker stems and even larger flowers of scarlet flushed lilac-purple (see p. 61), and *amecamensis*, prostrate with large pure white flowers.

Hildewintera see *Cleistocactus*

Lemaireocereus see *Pachycereus* and *Stenocereus*

Leuchtenbergia (Mexico)
L. principis, the sole member of the genus, is an extraordinary plant which looks like an agave. It has a quite small cylindrical body, but long, 3-angled, bluish green tubercles, often to 5 in. (12 cm) long, with paper-like spines at the tips. Flowers large, yellow, fragrant and long-lasting. Requires a loose, fairly rich soil and moderate watering in the growing season only.

Lobivia see *Echinopsis*

Lophocereus see *Pachycereus*

Lophophora (southern USA and Mexico)
Peyote, as it is called, yields a juice which is said to cause hallucinations. All are globular plants, dull bluish green, with a few obscure ribs and areoles with short tufts of hairs. An open sandy compost with a little lime added is advisable and they must be completely dry in winter.

L. williamsii, the type species, together with its varieties and the other two species, *L. lutea* and *L. diffusa*, are very similar. They have 7 to 10 ribs, low, rather indistinct tubercles and small pinkish or whitish flowers.

Machaerocereus see *Stenocereus*

Maihuenia (South America)
A small genus of rare plants from high altitudes in Chile and Patagonia (Argentina), which are remarkably frost-resistant. Stems are short, cylindrical, formed into dense low bushes, and have spines and persistent leaves. Flowers mostly terminal. *M. poeppigii* from Chile is a slow-growing species, stems to 2 in. (6 cm) long, oval, with 3 spines to each areole, persistent small leaves and pale yellow flowers to 1 in. (3 cm) long, the style with 10 green lobes.

Mamillopsis see *Mammillaria*

Mammillaria (Mexico, USA and West Indies)
One of the largest and most important genera of Cactaceae, containing nearly 200 species and numerous varieties. Plants mainly small-growing, normally offsetting freely, flowers fairly small but abundantly produced over a period of many weeks. A rich porous soil is necessary for them to thrive, together with good light, mostly full sun, and adequate watering in the growing season. Keep dry in winter.

M. blossfeldiana from Baja California is a solitary (as opposed to offsetting) species, with 15 to 20 radial spines and 3 to 4 centrals, black-tipped. Flowers are about $\frac{3}{4}$ in. (2 cm) wide, pale pinkish with a rich carmine central stripe. The variety *shurliana* is very similar, but the root system is bigger and the flowers whiter with the distinctive centre stripe.

M. *boolii* is found around San Carlos Bay in Sonora, Mexico, a dwarf species about 1 in. (3 cm) high and wide, clothed with numerous white radial spines and a longer central. Small flowers of lilac-purple form near the crown.

M. *elongata* from Hidalgo, Mexico, is very well known, with somewhat cylindrical stems which develop upright clusters. Spines variable, white, yellow, brown or darker. Flowers not prolific but fairly constant throughout the summer months, varying in colour from white to yellowish (see p. 44).

M. *hahniana* is an attractive white-spined hairy species from Guanajuato in Mexico at altitudes of nearly 6,500 ft (2,000 m). Plants $3\frac{1}{2}$ to $5\frac{1}{2}$ in. (9–14 cm) high, 4 in. (10 cm) thick, often grouping, with fine, long, whitish hairs densely covering the whole body. Flowers form around the crown of the plant, carmine-red. Flowering best in full sunlight.

M. *mystax* from Oaxaca, Mexico, grows to about 6 in. (15 cm) high and 4 in. (10 cm) wide, often developing offsets around the base. Stems greyish green covered with variously curved and twisting spines, tubercles 4-sided. Flowers numerous from around the crown, rich carmine-red, each about $\frac{3}{4}$ in. (2 cm) wide.

M. *oliviae* from Arizona, USA, is more or less globular and frequently offsets. Spines densely cover the stems, white or brownish. Flowers lilac-pink and purplish red, about 1 in. (3 cm) in diameter. Now considered a variety of M. *microcarpa*.

M. *prolifera*, originally from the West Indies, is apparently extinct there, but freely available in cultivation. It densely clusters, each stem to 2 in. (6 cm) long, $1\frac{1}{2}$ in. (4 cm) wide, with numerous hair-like spines and shorter dark central spines of reddish brown. Flowers creamy yellow with reddish brown central stripe, about $\frac{3}{4}$ in. (2 cm) long.

M. *senilis* (*Mamillopsis senilis*) is from Durango and Oaxaca in Mexico, often growing on limestone rock faces. Stems globular or oval, numerous whitish spines and flowers of orange-red or purplish with darker central stripe, to $2\frac{1}{2}$ in. (7 cm) long and 2 in. (6 cm) diameter, followed by large red-carmine fruits. A plant which nearly lost its identity when it ceased to have the status of a monotypic genus.

M. *zeilmanniana* from Guanajuato, Mexico, can be either solitary or forming tufts. Body dark green with many whitish, hair-like, radial spines and hooked, red-tipped, brownish centrals. Flowers are numerous and long-lasting, reddish purple. Ideal for the home (see p. 33).

Marginatocereus see *Pachycereus*

Mediolobivia see *Rebutia*

Melocactus (Mexico, West Indies, South America)
This is called the Turk's cap cactus because of the attractive hairy cap which develops on the crown. Globular plants, mostly with acute ribs and heavily spined. Flowers emerge from the cephalium. They require more attention than most cacti and a minimum of 65°F (18°C) is essential at all times, a rich soil with ample humus added, together with good drainage.

M. *bahiensis* from Brazil has a bluish green body to about 6 in. (15 cm) wide, 4 in. (10 cm) high, with a brownish bristly cephalium. Ribs 10 to 12. Flowers rose-pink.

M. *intortus* is from coastal areas of the West Indies. Plants to about $3\frac{1}{4}$ ft (1 m) high, thin ribs, and a long brownish cephalium capable of reaching 2 ft (60 cm) or more. Flowers perfectly cylindrical and pale pink, about $\frac{3}{4}$ in. (2 cm) long.

M. *matanzanus* from Cuba is a small species, about $3\frac{1}{2}$ in. (9 cm) wide, having a white hairy cephalium with brownish red bristles protruding. Small flowers carmine-red.

Monvillea see *Cereus*

Myrtillocactus (Mexico, Guatemala)

Tree-like plants, branching freely. Flowers are borne laterally, several to an areole. Fruits of some species are edible and when dried resemble raisins. An open compost with lime added makes a good growing medium.

M. geometrizens from central Mexico grows to about 13 ft (4 m) and has unusually bluish green stems to 4 in. (10 cm) thick. Few ribs and areoles set well apart with blackish spines. Flowers creamy yellow, fruits bluish.

Neobesseya see *Escobaria* and *Ortegocactus*

Neochilenia see *Neoporteria*

Neolloydia (Mexico, south USA)

A genus of globular or cylindrical plants with heavily spined tubercles. It now includes such well-known genera as *Gymnocactus*, *Echinomastus* and *Cuminaria*. A porous soil is essential, with full sun and a winter temperature not below 46°F (8°C).

N. conoidea is a variable species with a pale greyish green cylindrical stem to 4 in. (10 cm) high and oval tubercles, woolly axils and areoles bearing many whitish grey radial spines and longer black centrals. Flowers are reddish violet. The variety *grandiflora* is similar but with a larger, rich purple-pink or white flower to 1 in. (3 cm) long.

Neoporteria (South America)

A large genus which has absorbed several other genera, among them *Horridocactus*, *Islaya*, *Neochilenia* and *Pyrrhocactus*. Plants have globular or cylindrical stems with many ribs and several or few spines. They require an acid porous soil and a temperature no lower than 46°F (8°C), as many flower well into the winter.

N. subgibbosa from Chile becomes more elongated with maturity. Stems pale green with about 20 ribs, protruding chin-like tubercles and areoles with many sharp, erect, yellowish brown spines. Flowers are pinkish red, with a yellow tube, to 1½ in. (4 cm) long.

N. taltalensis (*Neochilenia taltalensis*) is globular to 3½ in. (8 cm) diameter, with about 12 bumpy ribs, up to 20 brown radial spines and usually 4 straight blackish centrals. Flowers creamy yellow, 1½ in. (3–4 cm) long. From Chile.

N. villosa, also from Chile, has greyish green stems, slightly tinged with purple, ribs spirally arranged with closely set white woolly areoles, yellow spines and long, bristly, erect hairs. Flowers are white, tipped pink, the tubes with reddish scales.

Notocactus see *Parodia*

Obregonia (Mexico)

A monotypic genus, perhaps closely related to *Strombocactus*.

O. denegrei is an unusual plant with a thick taproot, the globular stem about 3 to 4½ in. (8–12 cm) in diameter, greyish or dark green covered with many thick leaflike tubercles, which have areoles when young producing 2 to 4 bristly spines, but when older are spineless. Flowers 1 in. (3 cm) wide, white or pale pink. A rare desirable plant of fairly easy culture. It requires a very gritty compost and succeeds best in indirect light rather than full sun.

Opuntia (southern Canada to southern Argentina and West Indies)

A vast genus which now embraces several obsolete genera such as *Corynopuntia*, *Cylindropuntia*, *Austrocylindropuntia* and *Nopalea*. Stems or joints are pad-like or cylindrical. Some take several years to flower. The fruits of others are edible and known as prickly pears. In general they are of easy culture and a number are remarkably hardy. An open soil is essential, with full sun and generous watering during the growing period, but kept dry in winter.

O. fragilis from British Columbia, Canada, and Oregon and Washington, USA, is a small-growing species with cylindrical, spreading, almost prostrate joints, not exceeding 3 in. (8 cm) long, whitish green in colour. Brown to greyish spines and flowers of pale yellow about 2 in. (5 cm) across. This is an excellent rockery plant, but good drainage is essential.

O. humifusa, also known as *O. rafinesquei*, has rounded, flattish, oval, almost spine-

Above: *Heliocereus speciosus* var. *superbus* has outstanding rich-coloured flowers (see p.58)
Below left: *Echinopsis chamaecereus* is a valuable hardy cactus (see p.50)
Right: *Mammillaria hahniana* and other densely covered species prefer a warm sunny spot

less pads, often to 6 in. (15 cm) long. It is low-growing and spreading. Flowers are freely borne, sulphur-yellow, reddish at base of petals, followed by small pear-shaped fruits. May be grown outside.

O. hystricina is a variable species from the USA. The variety *bensonii*, better known as *O. rhodantha*, has large pad-like joints to 8 in. (20 cm) long and 3 in. (7–8 cm) wide, with 4 to 9 flattened greyish white spines and flowers of red, pink or white, each to over 2 in. (6 cm) across when open. Like *O. humifusa*, it is tolerant of most conditions including outdoors and is very decorative when in full bloom.

O. inarmata from Bolivia is a low-growing plant with small oval olive-green segments, covered with well spaced white areoles. Flowers bright to deep red to about 1½ in. (4 cm) across. A free-flowering, easily grown species.

O. lindheimeri (*O. aciculata*) from Texas, USA, has egg-shaped pads to 8 in. (20 cm) long, dark green, rounded at the top, and large bristly areoles. Spines brownish, tipped yellow, very slender. Flowers golden yellow to 4 in. (10 cm) in diameter. The variety *orbiculata* is similar, but the flowers are bright red.

O. microdasys and its varieties, all from north Mexico, are familiar to cactus lovers. The oval pads have a polka-dot effect, being symmetrically covered with well spaced areoles bearing sharp bristly glochids. Areoles can be yellow (var. *pallida*), white (var. *albispina*), or brownish red (var. *rufida*). Flowers pale yellow 1½ to 2 in. (4–5 cm) wide (see p. 51).

O. phaeacantha is another species from the USA. Some varieties are hardy, notably *O. phaeacantha camanchica*, which has large, clear green, oval joints to 6 in. (15 cm) long, whitish spines and large yellow or reddish flowers 2½ to 3½ in. (6–9 cm) across. A very attractive plant, but the rootstock should be kept very dry in winter.

O. polyacantha from British Columbia and many parts of the USA is prostrate and very variable. The pad-like joints are about 4 in. (10 cm) long, 2½ to 3 in. (7–8 cm) wide, rather thin, pale green in colour and with many spines. Flowers are pale yellow to orange, to about 2½ in. (7 cm) across. This also accepts quite unpleasant weather conditions, given good drainage.

O. pycnantha from Baja California is a much sought-after species with oblong pads to 8 in. (20 cm) long, hairy and spiny. Large closely set areoles with yellowish glochids and spines. Flowers pale to bright yellow, about 1½ in. (4 cm) wide. There is also a delightful cristate form, with elegantly twisted and curled joints.

O. rastrera, a prostrate, creeping species from Mexico, has joints about 8 in. (20 cm) long, egg-shaped and very spiny and numerous yellow glochids. Flowers are pale to deep yellow. Does well if planted outside under a projecting roof and is very frost-resistant, but less satisfactory if the soil becomes too wet.

O. spegazzini from west Argentina grows to about 3¼ ft (1 m) high, with branches to 1 in. (3 cm) thick, smooth with small areoles. Spines few, flowers white, small, followed by reddish fruits.

Oreocereus (South America)

A small genus with large areoles, many spines and long hairs. They are decorative and suited for home or greenhouse. A good sunny position, an open rich soil which includes humus and lime, plus regular watering in summer and monthly fertilizing in the growing season will ensure robust growth.

O. celsiana and its several varieties are all spectacular plants, differing only in spine and hair colouring. The typical species has yellow spines, brownish white hairs and red flowers. Variety *trollii* has white hairs, yellow spines and carmine-red flowers; the variety *ritteri* is of more slender growth, with yellowish brown spines and hairs and an orange-red flower; and variety *fossulatus* has pale yellow spines and red flowers.

O. hempelianus (*Arequipa weingartiana*) from high altitudes in Chile grows to about 1¼ ft (40 cm) tall and 4 in. (10 cm) wide, greyish green with pronounced ribs and heavily spined. Flowers from the crown, orange-red, somewhat tubular in shape to about 2 in. (5 cm) long.

O. leucotrichus (*Arequipa leucotricha*) from Chile grows to 2 ft (60 cm), with humped ribs, densely woolly at the top. Flowers red, about 3 in. (7–8 cm) long, 1 in. (3 cm) wide. An attractive sought-after species.

Oroya (Peru)
A small genus of semi-globose plants with numerous ribs and spines completely clothing the stem. Flowers are borne around or near the crown. They are high altitude plants, requiring cool conditions in winter and a warm position in summer. An acid porous soil is essential and the more nutritious the better.

O. borchersii is light green in colour with brownish yellow spines completely enveloping the body in comb-like formation. Flowers bright yellow, about 1 in. (3 cm) long.

O. peruviana has a deep green body to 4 in. (10 cm) high, 6 in. (15 cm) wide. Areoles with whitish wool and about 20 brown spines and few whitish hairs. Flowers about 1 in. (3 cm) long, orange-red.

Ortegocactus
A small genus closely allied to *Escobaria*. The globular stems are very small with prominent tubercules which are decidedly furrowed. It needs full sun and a mineral-based compost.

O. macdougalii (*Neobesseya macdougalii*) is a miniature, greyish blue, globular species, with blackish spines and pure yellow flowers 1 in. (2–3 cm) long. A choice and desirable plant which requires a minimum temperature of 54°F (12°C) at all times.

Pachycereus (Mexico)
There are several species, all big plants and including some of the largest of the Cactaceae. In maturity they become tree-like, with a shorter trunk and many ascending branches. They need a good sunny position, porous soil, plenty of water in summer and to be kept dry in winter. Young plants are useful for home or greenhouse and are slow-growing.

P. marginatus (*Stenocereus* (*Marginatocereus*) *marginatus*) from Mexico is a tree-forming species, with dark greyish green stems to 20 ft (6 m) high, 1 ft (30 cm) thick in the wild. Areoles very closely set, almost meeting, spines reddish, soon falling off. Flowers reddish externally, white internally, 1½ to 2 in. (4–5 cm) long.

P. militaris (*Backebergia militaris*) is a spectacular columnar plant with a large, rounded brush-like cephalium of long, brown, bristly hairs which looks like a busby. It grows to 19 ft (6 m) in height and about 4 in. (10 cm) thick and has very pronounced ribs with areolas bearing several greyish spines. Flowers reddish orange protruding from the cephalium (see p. 48).

P. pringlei reaches 40 ft (12 m) high in the wild and is distinctly tree-like, robust, the stems and branches with about 15 obtuse ribs, brown-felted areoles and many black-tipped spines. Flowers appear only on mature plants, whitish, about 3 in. (8 cm) long, the tube scaly and hairy. Cristate forms occur very occasionally and these have to be seen to be believed.

P. schottii (*Lophocereus schottii*) has dull green stems about 2 in. (6 cm) thick and to about 3¼ ft (1 m) high, often to 15 ft (5 m) in the wild. Spines 5 to 7, blackish or greyish and very short. Flowers appear through the cephalium, 1½–2 in. (4–5 cm) long with a short tube, reddish with white stamens, greenish externally. It likes a semi-shady position but is slow-growing. There is also a choice monstrose form, known as the totem pole because of its peculiar shape.

P. weberi (*Lemaireocereus weberi*) is a tree-like species to 32 ft (10 m) tall in the wild. It has a dark blue-green stem, long blackish spines and creamy white flowers.

Parodia (South America)
A genus of very many species, mostly small globose plants, usually solitary but sometimes offsetting. They make good house plants, requiring a bright location,

regular watering and feeding in warm weather and, if a minimum temperature of 50°F (10°C) can be maintained, slight moisture in winter. A soil enriched with humus and very open is necessary for best results.

P. alacriportana (*P. brevihamata*) from Brazil is a small plant, only 1½ in. (3–4 cm) wide, olive-green in colour and having about 22 ribs with tubercles spirally arranged. Areoles white, woolly, bearing yellowish spines, the centrals with brownish tips. Flowers are large, golden yellow.

P. brevihamata (*Notocactus brevihamatus*) is a small-growing plant to 3½ in. (8 cm) thick, rather globular in shape and offsetting at the base. Spines about 20, yellowish brown, from closely set areoles, and golden yellow flowers about 1½ in. (4 cm) wide. From Rio Grande do Sul, Brazil.

P. crassigibba (*Notocactus uebelmannianus*) is globular, about 5 to 6 in. (12–15 cm) in diameter, with many rounded ribs and fine greyish white spines becoming pale brown. Flowers reddish purple, about 1½ in. (4 cm) long from the crown of the plant. Native of Brazil.

P. herteri (*Notocactus herteri*) A globular species about 6 in. (15 cm) in diameter, from Brazil and Uruguay. It has about 20 ribs bearing 8–11 radial spines, 4–6 centrals, often to ¾ in. (2 cm) long. The crown has white woolly spots and is spineless. Flowers reddish purple, sometimes in much paler shades.

P. leninghausii (*Notocactus leninghausii*) has a columnar stem, slightly flattened and slanting on top. Spines numerous, golden yellow, hair-like, from closely set areoles. Large golden yellow flowers, about 1½ in. (4 cm) long, appear in the crown and are long-lasting. From Brazil (see p. 33).

P. magnifica (*Notocactus magnificus*) also from Brazil, is more globular and often freely offsetting, with very pronounced ribs and numerous white spines, the centrals more brownish. Flowers bright yellow, 2 in. (5 cm) long and wide (see p. 68).

P. microsperma (*P. mutabilis*) from Argentina is a globular plant to about 3 in. (8 cm) thick, the ribs divided into tubercles. Large woolly areoles with about 50 fine whitish spines and 4 brownish hooked centrals. Flowers are yellow, sometimes with a red throat, up to 1½ in. (4 cm) wide.

P. schwebsiana from Bolivia reaches to 5½ in. (14 cm) high and 4½ in. (11 cm) thick. Ribs 13 to 20, slightly spiralled, with close-set, white, woolly areoles and yellowish brown radial and central spines. A beautiful species with blood-red flowers 1 in. (3 cm) across.

P. scopa (*Notocactus scopa*) is cylindrical in form. Spines whitish, sometimes reddish-tipped. Flowers borne in a circle around the crown, canary yellow with a red stigma. From Brazil and Uruguay.

P. stuemeri (*P. setosa*) from north Argentina grows to about 10 in. (25 cm) high and 5 in. (12 cm) wide. The stem is dark green and woolly with about 35 ribs bearing areoles with about 40 spines. Flowers appear in the crown of the plant, rich carmine-red.

Pelecyphora (Mexico)

P. strobiliformis (*Encephalocarpus strobiloformis*), the sole species, resembles a fir cone in its appearance. It is a globular plant, 1½ to 2 in. (4–6 cm) across, with regularly arranged tubercles greyish green and scale-like and an areole on the inner side of each. Flowers are borne from the crown of the plant on the young tubercles, violet-red, 1 to 1½ in. (3–4 cm) wide, the petals fringed at the tips, yellow style and stamens. A porous soil is essential for this greatly sought-after plant and it needs extreme care in cultivation (see p.53).

Pereskia (Mexico, Bolivia, Peru)

Mostly vine-like plants, often developing tree-like proportions, but invariably clambering. Stems long, slender and bearing true leaves. Spiny and free-flowering, they are excellent for growing in the greenhouse. A rich open compost is advisable and a minimum temperature of 50°F (10°C). Cuttings of unflowered year-old terminal

branches, taken in April and May, make good grafting stock for other cacti.
P. aculeata, widespread in southern USA, West Indies and South America, is a
climbing clambering species with stems to 33 ft (10 m) long in its native habitat and
even in cultivation if space permits. Freely branching with elliptical dark green
leaves and sweetly scented, creamy yellow flowers in clusters. A fully developed
plant will produce flowers in profusion (see p. 21).
P. grandifolia from Colombia and Brazil is close to and possibly synonymous with
P. bleo. A shrub-like species with large oblong leaves, rather spiny, and very lovely
lilac-rose or pinkish flowers from the tips of the branches.

Pilosocereus (Mexico, USA, West Indies, South America)
A genus of some 50 species of tall columnar plants which develop a hairy cephalium
with maturity. Not difficult in cultivation, given liberal watering in the growing
season, a porous soil rich in humus, and a minimum winter temperature of 45°F
(7°C).
P. glaucescens is a tall erect species from Brazil, with bluish green stems, rounded
ribs, close-set areoles with many white bristles and hairs, spines yellowish brown.
Currently classified as *Pseudopilosocereus glaucescens*.
P. leucocephalus (*P. palmeri*) from east Mexico has stout bluish green stems, about
3 in. (8 cm) thick, and 8 to 9 prominent ribs regularly set with white woolly areoles,
armed with spines. The apex becomes densely woolly after a few years, through
which appear nocturnal reddish whitish flowers to 3 in. (8 cm) long, 2 in. (5 cm)
wide.

Pterocactus (Argentina)
A genus of 7 species, close to *Opuntia*. They form a large tuberous root system and
have wide-winged seeds, a peculiar feature found only in this genus. Fairly easy
plants to grow, they can also be grafted on *Opuntia* stock.
P. knutzei (*P. tuberosus*) has thin brownish green stems, cylindrical and covered
with numerous minute, whitish, hairy spines. Flowers are bright yellow, about 1 in.
(3 cm) in diameter.

Rebutia (South America)
A genus of very many species, globular or rarely short cylindrical plants which
cluster freely. They have no distinctive ribs, but regularly arranged small tubercles.
Of easy culture, requiring a rich porous soil and semi-shade rather than full sun.
Regular watering and feeding periodically during the growing season will ensure
good flowering. Excellent for home or greenhouse.
R. arenacea (*Sulcorebutia menesesii*) has rather bristly pinkish white spines set
comb-like from the slightly elongated areoles. Flowers yellow.
R. aureiflora (*Mediolobivia aureiflora*) has a dark purplish green body and clusters
freely. Whitish areoles bearing up to 16 radial spines and 4 centrals. Flowers
variable in colour, either a rich orange-yellow, or pink in the form *kesselringiana*, or
deep red in the form *sarothroides*. Native of Argentina.
R. heliosa is an unusual species, the dark greenish globular body, either solitary or
offsetting, completely obliterated by a dense covering of small tubercles and minute
whitish spines. Flowers are bright orange, to 2 in. (5 cm) long, 1½ in. (4 cm) wide,
with the suggestion of a whitish throat. It is from Bolivia. Needs careful cultivation
and a permeable rich soil for the tap-root.
R. marsoneri from north Argentina has a dark green body, many yellowish brown
spines and pale to deep yellow flowers.
R. minuscula (*R. senilis*) in the form *kesselringiana* also bears yellow flowers. The
globular body has many longish white hairs and spines (see p. 33).
R. multispina (*Weingartia multispina*) is a Bolivian species, globular, to about 5½ in.
(14 cm) diameter, greyish green, with slightly elongated areoles bearing 25 to 30
whitish spines. Flowers golden yellow, appearing from around the sides of the
plant.

R. neocumingii (*Weingartia neocumingii*) from Peru could be synonymous with *W. cumingii*, for there seems little to distinguish them. Bright green globular body, ribs divided into oval tubercles, woolly areoles bearing many whitish to brownish yellow spines. Flowers golden yellow or orange-yellow from near the apex of the plant.

R. pulvinosa (*R. albiflora*) from Bolivia is a many-clustering species, the body globular with about 15 radial spines and up to 5 centrals. Flowers white with a pinkish stripe, about 1 in. (3 cm) wide.

R. steinbachii (*Sulcorebutia glomerispina*, *S. taratensii*) attains about 2 in. (5 cm) high and wide, the bluish green body surrounded with 24 ribs. Radial spines 12 to 15, whitish or deep orange-yellowish, to about ¾ in. (2 cm) long. Flowers reddish-purple, up to 1 in. (3 cm) long.

Stenocactus (Mexico)
Globular plants with thin, wavy, deeply grooved ribs. Spines are usually long and somewhat flattened, often forming an entangled mass at the crown. Sun-loving and requiring a very well-drained soil and frequent watering during the growing season. The genus was formerly known as *Echinofossulocactus*.

S. coptonogonus (*Echinofossulocactus coptonogonus*) has only about 14 deeply notched ribs, with areoles set well apart and soft, straw-coloured, incurved, flattened spines. Flowers variable in colour, white to purple with mauvish red centres, 1 to 1½ in. (3–4 cm) long and wide.

S. crispatus (*Echinofossulocactus violaciflorus*) has about 35 wavy thin ribs with roundish areoles set well apart bearing a few curved yellowish grey spines. Flowers about 1 in. (2–3 cm) long, white with a purple median line, the style and stamens deep violet.

S. multicostatus (*Echinofossulocactus multicostatus*) has over 100 thin, closely set, wavy ribs, each with 2 to 3 areoles bearing a few elongated, flexible, erect, spreading spines. Flowers about 1 in. (2–3 cm) long, white or pinkish white with a pale purplish centre.

S. vaupelianus (*Echinofossulocactus vaupelianus*) is a globular solitary plant, about 3½ in. (9 cm) tall and wide, dull green in colour, the crown being densely covered with white wool and brownish spines. Ribs 30 to 40, wavy, the woolly areoles bearing 20 or more needle-like spines, white to brownish. Flowers creamy yellow or white, about 1 in. (2 cm) long.

Stenocereus (USA and Mexico)
A relatively small genus which has been enlarged by the addition of species of *Lemaireocereus*, *Marginatocereus*, *Ritterocereus* and *Machaerocereus*. Columnar or tree-like plants with few or many ribs. Flowers are usually borne from near the apex of the stems, mostly nocturnal and scaly or felted externally. Of easy culture, generally slow-growing. The genus also now includes the rare and demanding *S. eruca* (*Machaeocereus eruca*) or creeping devil.

S. thurberi (*Lemaireocereus thurberi*) has a wide distribution in Arizona and north Mexico. A stout much-branched plant forming clumps, each growing several feet high in their native habitat. Stems dark brownish green, low ribs and large brown felted areoles bearing up to 10 radial spines and 1 to 3 centrals, all dark brown. Flowers at the tips of the branches, pink with whitish margins, about 2½ in. (7 cm) long (see p. 16).

Stetsonia (Argentina)
S. coryne, the sole species, is a tree-like plant with bluish green stems, 7 to 9 obtuse ribs and woolly areoles with blackish spines of unequal length creating a spectacular effect. Flowers nocturnal, white, glossy green externally to 6 in. (15 cm) long, appearing from the sides of the stem. A popular plant in cultivation, requiring well drained soil rich in humus, a sunny location, moderate watering in the growing season, otherwise kept dry, and a minimum temperature of 50°F (10°C).

Strombocactus (Mexico)

A small genus closely allied to *Turbinocarpus* and by some thought inseparable. Globular plants completely covered with flattened tubercles and with only few spines, which soon fall off. They need a very gritty, enriched compost, a position in full sun and should be watered in moderation in summer and kept completely dry in winter.

S. *disciformis* is greyish green, compressed and with flattened, closely set tubercles in 12 to 18 rows. Flowers white to yellowish, about 1 in. (3 cm) long, 1½ in. (4 cm) across, appear in the crown.

Sulcorebutia see *Rebutia*

Thelocactus (Mexico and USA)

A genus of colourful, globular, spiny plants, about 28 in number, all easy to grow. They are sun-lovers, requiring a moderately rich, porous compost, and best suited for greenhouse culture.

T. *bicolor* from Texas to central Mexico has slightly spiralled ribs, long spines with even longer centrals and large bright flowers to 2 in. (6 cm) long, purplish pink or red. This and its varieties are now considered *Ferocactus*.

T. *rinconensis* (T. *lophothele*) is a long globular plant to about 8 in. (20 cm) high with a rather sunken crown. The ribs, 15 to 20 in number, are slender with pronounced tubercles. Spines few, curved, yellowish, sometimes with one very long central. Flowers pale yellow internally, green with reddish stripes on outer surface. From Chihuahua, north Mexico.

T. *setispinus* (*Hamatocactus setispinus*) is globular to about 6 in. (15 cm) tall, 4 in. (10 cm) wide, having brown or white spines with a hooked central one. Flowers yellow with reddish centre, 2½ in. (6–7 cm) long. From southern Texas and neighbouring Mexico.

T. *tulensis* is a Mexican species, semi-globular or short and cylindrical to 5 in. (12 cm) high and 4 in. (10 cm) thick. Areoles elliptical, set well apart with a woolly section just above each one. Spines brown, the radial 6 to 8 and spreading and long centrals, if any, to 1 in. (3 cm) long. Flowers pink with deeper lined central stripe to 1 in. (3 cm) long.

Trichocereus see *Echinopsis*

Turbinocarpus (Mexico)

A small genus which has absorbed other genera such as *Toumeya* and *Normanbokea* and is also close or identical to *Strombocactus*. These are colourful miniatures, the body varying in colour from green or bluish green to brownish. Globular plants, solitary, with papery spination and colourful flowers. They are relatively easy to grow, but an open rich soil is essential, with the addition of lime. They require a bright but not sunny position.

T. *lophophoroides*, so named because of its resemblance to species of *Lophophora*, grows to about 1 in. (3 cm) high, 1½ in. (4 cm) wide and has a pale greenish body with 2 to 6 light brown or black spines. Flowers white or pinkish, about 1 in. (3 cm) wide, appearing from the white woolly crown.

T. *valdezianus* is oval globular, about 1 in. (3 cm) wide, growing from a long taproot. Body bluish green, areoles with numerous white, hair-like, miniature spines. Flowers white or lilac-pink, about 1 in. (3 cm) wide.

T. *viereckii* (*Neolloydia viereckii*) has a short globular stem to 2 in. (6 cm) diameter, rarely clustering. Tubercles set in about 15 rows, the upper part of the stem densely white woolly, with many long whitish radial spines and 4 black-tipped centrals. Flowers rose or lilac-pink, widely spreading, about ¾ in. (2 cm) long.

Uebelmannia (South America)

A genus of some 6 species which have recently attracted the attention of collectors. They are globular or semi-cylindrical, with peculiar formations of the body. A rich porous soil is necessary and they should be carefully watered during the growing

Above left: *Escobaria asperispina*, showing the genus's distinctive flowers (see p.52)
Above right: *Parodia magnifica*, rewarding and easily grown (see p.64)
Below: *Opuntia microdasys*, a common species in this extensive genus (see p.62)

Echinocereus leucanthus is often best grown as a grafted plant (see p.49)

season and then kept dry. A minimum temperature of 50 to 55°F (10–12°C) is required, higher if possible.

U. gummifera from Brazil has a dull greyish green body to $4\frac{1}{2}$ in. (12 cm) high, 2 in. (6 cm) wide, with over 30 tubercled ribs and up to 7 spines, greyish with brown tip. The two central spines point one up and one down. Flowers small, yellow, appearing in the crown.

U. pectinifera has a dark reddish brown body entirely covered with whitish scales, giving it the effect of being greyish blue. Ribs about 16, closely set and bearing black spines, perpendicularly arranged, like the teeth of a comb. Areoles in crown felted with greyish wool, from whence the small yellow flowers appear.

Weingartia *see Rebutia*
Wilcoxia *see Echinocereus*

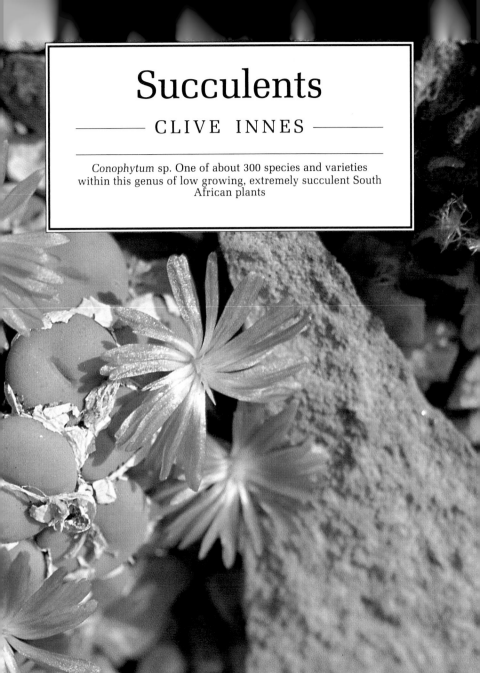

Succulents

─── CLIVE INNES ───

Conophytum sp. One of about 300 species and varieties within this genus of low growing, extremely succulent South African plants

Above: *Agave victoriae-reginae* is one of the finest species in the genus
Below: The hybrids of *Portulaca grandiflora* make a colourful addition to any garden

Introduction

The plants commonly termed 'succulents' are so numerous that it would prove a mammoth task even to consider an introduction to them all. Over 50 different plant families include genera in which succulents are represented, with about 12 families containing the more familiar and easily available species. This section, therefore, concentrates on those succulents most likely to be encountered, with the major exception of cacti, which are dealt with in the first section of this book. The Cactaceae, although it is one of the four main families of succulents, is distinguished from all the others by having a peculiar growing point called an areole, a small cushion-like growth from which develop spines, flowers and branches.

Many succulents have an unusual appearance and are often confused with cacti – an understandable mistake when one considers the resemblance of several euphorbias to cacti. It is hoped that this section will be useful in explaining any particular characteristics which help to identify succulents and that in general it will provide enough basic information to enable the beginner to grow these very attractive plants successfully.

Succulents are decorative, adaptable, not difficult culturally and can be a pleasant addition to the home. Equally, in a greenhouse they can ensure a colourful and intriguing display throughout the year. They have a place in the garden too. Many species are relatively hardy in Britain and some, notably sedums and sempervivums, are commonly grown as alpines in gardens. Other well-known succulents are the annual *Portulaca grandiflora* in its many coloured forms and the Livingstone daisy, *Dorotheanthus bellidiformis*, whose decorative flowers adorn gardens during the summer months. We have become accustomed to seeing the yucca as a garden plant and the agave also, particularly in southern Britain.

Conservation and the need to ensure the survival of plants in their habitat have at last gained well-deserved prominence. It is worthy of note that many succulents which find their way into cultivation, for instance, *Euphorbia obesa*, *Luckhoffia* and *Aloe variegata*, are almost extinct in the wild. It is the duty of those who possess such plants to treasure them and propagate them, so that they are not lost to posterity. Fortunately, numerous societies exist

Luckhoffia beukmanii, from Cape Province, South Africa, has become very rare in its native habitat

worldwide to encourage interest in succulents and promote their conservation, including the British Cactus and Succulent Society, which is open to all enthusiasts. Nature reserves and national and regional parks have also become a necessary and welcome feature in countries where succulent plant populations were being decimated.

The growing of succulents can become an absorbing hobby, but it is necessary to take certain precautions. Never buy a plant just for the name: names change often and you could well discover that your purchase is already in your collection under another label. When buying a plant, examine it thoroughly and make sure it is in good condition – free from pests, clean-looking and not pale and straggly. There are many specialist nurseries and reputable plant centres which stock a wide range of succulents and they frequently offer a mail-order service, if you cannot visit in person. Seed of named species is also obtainable from a number of sources.

What Is a Succulent?

Broadly defined, a succulent is a plant capable of withstanding long periods of drought. It is equipped to survive such adverse conditions by the ability to store moisture – in the leaves, the stem or the rootstock – and this feature is evident in all the thousands of succulent plants now known.

LEAF SUCCULENTS

In these species, nearly the whole leaf constitutes the water storage tissue and is entirely enveloped in a thin layer of assimilating tissue, for absorbing water and carbon dioxide and converting them to food. With certain of the family Mesembryanthemaceae, the leaf structure has been reduced to a small evaporative area, often with just two 'leaves' almost fused together in a rounded fleshy body, as in *Lithops* and *Conophytum*. With other genera, such as *Echeveria*, *Aloe* and *Agave*, the fleshy leaves have become more or less compacted in the form of a rosette, thus affording protection from the evaporating effect of the rays of the sun. Finally, with succulents like *Crassula* and *Kalanchoe*, the leaves may be set at intervals along the stems and are noticeably fleshy, with a coating of tough wax-like skin to discourage evaporation.

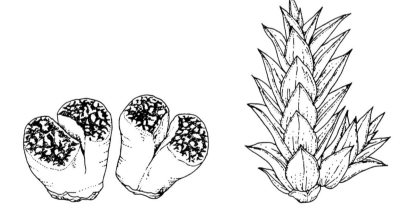

Examples of leaf succulents – *Lithops* (left) and *Haworthia viscosa* (right)

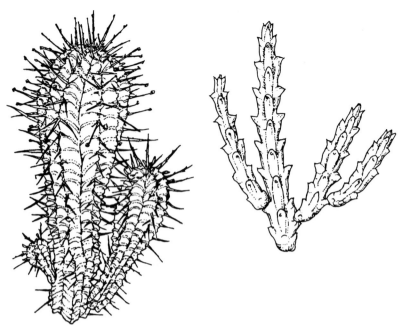

Examples of stem succulents – *Euphorbia horrida* (left) and *Orbea* (Stapelia) *variegata* (right)

STEM SUCCULENTS

These plants are generally almost or totally leafless and what leaves they have tend to fall quickly. The absence of leaves actually provides against transpiration or loss of moisture through evaporation. Leafless succulents are invariably of very fleshy texture and the water storage tissue is concentrated in the fresh green stems and shoots (and also in the small leaves which may develop temporarily in some species). Hence, the functions of transpiration and assimilation, which are normally undertaken by the leaves, are the prime responsibility of the shoots and stems, so guaranteeing the survival of the plant. Many stem succulents have angled shoots, for instance, *Euphorbia*, *Stapelia* and *Caralluma*, as an additional precaution against excessive evaporation; the shoots not only have the protective skin, but with some species there is also a fine wax-like covering or a coating of minute hairs.

ROOT SUCCULENTS

These succulents have a thick, fleshy, mostly tuberous rootstock, which provides a reservoir of nourishment for the plant. The tuberous roots may be large, small round or elongated, the latter often in the form of a lengthy taproot, although a few plants, for example, *Boweia*, possess more of a bulbous base. With all these succulents, the water storage tissue is mainly confined to the rootstock. In certain cases, such as *Pachypodium*, the stems arise directly from the tuberous rootstock. This often develops into a thick, fleshy, rounded, swollen base at, or slightly below, ground level, which is termed a caudex. The caudex may be coated with a thick tough skin, or frequently has a corky or woody surface, protecting the water storage tissue and enabling the plant to

Example of root succulents – *Ceropegia woodii*

Left: The stems of *Pachypodium rosulatum* var. *gracilis* emerge directly from the caudex
Right: *Euphorbia milii*, the crown of thorns, is one of the best known representatives of the genus

withstand long periods of drought. Many of the Cucurbitaceae family have distinctive caudices and there is something of a 'caudiciform cult' among enthusiasts for these unusual plants.

DISTRIBUTION

Succulents have a worldwide distribution. Some — *Sedum*, *Sempervivum*, *Chiastophyllum* and the like – are to be found in northern Europe. More are encountered in temperate zones of southern Europe, parts of China and Japan, notably *Orostachys*, a few *Caralluma*, many *Sedum* and other low-growing plants. By far the greatest number, however, inhabit the tropical and subtropical regions of the world and species of the same genus are often widely dispersed across them. Thus *Kalanchoe* is native to Africa, including Madagascar, as well as the West Indies and other areas of the New World, while *Euphorbia* is represented on every continent, the obvious characteristics of shape, size and general structure varying according to habitat. Members of the family Asclepiadaceae abound from the Himalayan regions to parts of Australia, with *Hoya* species at the two extremes, and there are untold species of *Stapelia*, *Caralluma*, *Huernia*, *Hoodia*, *Ceropegia* and other genera in the vast African complex between.

The Americas are basically the home of *Agave, Yucca, Echeveria, Dudleya* and several other popular genera and even a number of *Sedum* species occur in the USA and Mexico. *Jatropha* are virtually confined to America and the West Indies. Africa in its entirety houses the majority of succulent plants and many of them, such as *Aloe, Haworthia* and *Gasteria*, are found only there. The numerous species within the family Mesembryanthemaceae are almost exclusive to Africa, with a very few exceptions in Australia and elsewhere. The genus *Pelargonium* too is largely African, most of the species being from the south of the country.

A knowledge of the habitats of succulent plants – the rainy and dry seasons that they experience, the altitudes at which they grow, their flowering periods and whether they have to accept long periods of drought or enjoy more kindly conditions during the year – is helpful in understanding how to care for them in cultivation. The most important factor in successful growing is to really know your plants.

Xanthorrhoea semiplana (now included within the new family Xanthorrhoea-ceae) grows very large in its natural habitat

Cultivation

There are certain guidelines to follow when growing succulent plants, whether in the home or greenhouse, or even outdoors (see p. 84).

COMPOST

With very few exceptions, a mixture composed of these ingredients (by volume) will achieve good results:

1 part good sterilized loam
2 parts finely shredded sphagnum peat
1 part sharp, gritty, washed sand
plus a sprinkling of slow-release fertilizer or, even better, a little thoroughly decomposed cow manure

Unfortunately, good uncontaminated loam is now scarce and expensive. The alternative to the home-made mixture is to buy a specially prepared cactus compost or a commercially produced soilless compost. The cactus compost is equally suitable for most other succulents and should already contain sufficient gritty sand, but if it seems too retentive of moisture, add a little more. With soilless compost it is necessary to incorporate small, washed, gritty sand, to make up a third or slightly more of the total bulk. It is also possible to use John Innes potting compost No. 2, again providing additional washed, gritty sand.

It is essential to include gritty sand in the compost in order to obtain a very porous mixture, for succulents cannot tolerate wet feet and will quickly rot.

WATERING

Succulents should be watered only during the period of active growth, which varies according to the plant concerned. Water the compost thoroughly when it is dry, then wait until it is almost dried out again before giving more water. Little doses, whether the plant needs it or not, can be harmful. Remember that no water is required during the dormant season. Generally speaking, this coincides with the winter months in Britain, from early November to March, although there are exceptions, as noted in the Directory (pp. 90–120).

FEEDING

The supply of nutrients in a prepared compost lasts for a limited time and succulents should therefore be fed at roughly monthly intervals during the growing and flowering seasons. General-purpose fertilizers, containing nitrogen and potash, as well as the essential trace elements like iron, magnesium, manganese, boron, copper and molybdenum, are suitable. They are available in liquid form or as a soluble powder to be added to the water.

CONTAINERS

Clay or plastic containers may be used, although plastic has the advantage of being easier to keep clean and tends to dry out less rapidly than clay. The size of pot is important and should be selected to allow room for the roots of the plant to spread without being cramped or, in the case of a plant with a taproot, to provide sufficient depth for root growth. If a plant is under-potted, it will soon begin struggling. At the other extreme, if it is over-potted, the plant may look ridiculous and can have too much damp soil around the rootstock during the growing season, which inhibits the drying-out process. Always crock the container well, placing a layer of broken pot, gravel or similar material at the bottom to assist drainage.

Repotting is required only when the roots start to protrude through the base of the pot or become very obvious on the surface of the compost. It is usually best carried out in early spring.

LIGHT

Most succulents will take full sun or, at least, bright light, although there are exceptions (see the Directory, p. 90). As before, it helps to know something about their origin – whether from open arid country, like most of the Mesembryanthemaceae family, or protected from the blistering effect of the sun's rays by other plant life, as with members of the Commelinaceae – so that you can place them in the best position.

TEMPERATURE

It is wise to maintain a minimum temperature of 55°F (13°C) for the majority of succulents and with many of them a slightly higher temperature will prove beneficial.

Succulents for Different Situations

IN THE HOME

A number of succulents have had a place of honour as houseplants for very many years, often without the owner even being aware they were succulents. *Hoya* and *Sansevieria* are two which come to mind; there are also the partridge-breasted aloe, *Aloe variegata*, and the numerous hybrids of *Kalanchoe blossfeldiana*, with their long-lasting flowers in many beautiful shades, which have become popular more recently. However, the majority of succulent plants, not just a chosen few, can be grown very successfully indoors, so long as they are given a bright position, away from draughts, and normal procedures for watering and feeding are followed.

One other point may be mentioned: it is often assumed that plants should be watered from below, standing the pot in water until it has taken its fill. This can be done, always remembering to tip away any surplus water afterwards, but it is not really necessary. Plants can just as easily be watered from above, which also helps to keep them free from dust. Do not water in the heat of the day, when there is a danger of burns from the combination of sunshine and drops of water on the plants.

IN THE GREENHOUSE

Those who have the benefit of a greenhouse can provide ideal conditions for growing succulents, especially some of the larger ones which may be difficult to accommodate in the home. First and foremost, the greenhouse must be sound and weatherproof and free from draughts. Good ventilation is essential to prevent stagnation and can be achieved with roof and side vents. Fans can be introduced if necessary to improve the air circulation.

Succulents must have good light throughout the year and therefore the greenhouse should be in an open sunny location and the glass must be kept really clean. However, certain species need protection from full sun, otherwise they might be scorched, and

Above: *Kalanchoe blossfeldiana* is familiar as a houseplant
Below: The beauty of the Mesembryanthemaceae, one of the largest succulent families

should have some sort of shading, for instance, green netting, slats or white shading painted on the outside of the glass. Heating will be required to maintain the correct temperature. The safest and most efficient system for a small greenhouse is an electrically controlled convector, which distributes warm air to every corner of the structure and does not emit harmful fumes. (See also the Wisley Handbook, *The Small Greenhouse*.)

OUTDOORS

A number of succulents can be successfully grown outdoors, particularly sedums and sempervivums, most of which are completely hardy. They are popular alpine plants and do well in a rock garden, raised bed or trough. The well-known century plant, *Agave americana*, also thrives in gardens in the mild south and west of Britain; in colder districts it may be grown in a large container and placed outside in the summer. Yuccas can be treated in the same way. As bedding plants raised from seed, *Dorotheanthus bellidiformis* and *Portulaca grandiflora* provide carpets of colour in a sunny flower bed.

Succulents grown outdoors are best planted on a slope, to maximize drainage, in a sunny open position. They appreciate some protection from wind and rain and can be placed against a south-facing wall or, better still, in the shelter of a roof overhang. Garden soil usually meets their requirements, especially if it is reasonably light and porous.

Most pot-grown succulents will benefit from a period in the open air. Choose a time in late spring or summer when the weather is congenial and place them, still in their pots, in a light draught-free position outside, though not necessarily in full sun. Remember that they will need regular watering.

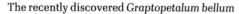

The recently discovered *Graptopetalum bellum*

Propagation

There are several ways to increase a collection of succulents, all of which present very few obstacles.

SEED

Seed is the obvious first choice and is a particularly useful method with some of the less common species, which are not so readily available as plants from commercial sources. It has the further merit of being economical and of producing plants which, from the moment of germination, become adjusted to the conditions on which they will be grown. With due care, seed-grown plants can make excellent mature specimens, so long as their essential requirements are met.

To prepare for sowing, select a suitable seed tray or pot, completely cover the base with a shallow layer of small gravel to prevent waterlogging and fill with a gritty seed compost to within $\frac{1}{2}$ in. (1 cm) of the top. Firm well to make a level surface. For very fine, almost dust-like seeds, spread a thin layer of sharp small grit over the compost surface and carefully sprinkle the seeds on top, but do not cover the compost. Larger seeds should be set on top of the prepared compost and covered with a layer of gritty sand the same depth as the size of the seeds. Then lightly spray the compost, using tepid water if possible, until it is evenly moist; alternatively, stand the seed tray in a bowl of tepid water until the surface of the compost is visibly moist and allow it to drain. Cover with a sheet of glass, paper or both and keep in a semi-shady but warm place, in a heated propagator if available. Generally speaking, a temperature of 70°F (21°C) is sufficient throughout the germination period. Germination may take only a few days, or sometimes weeks, even months, so don't despair if seeds fail to produce results as quickly as you hoped!

Once the seeds have germinated, remove the glass, but leave the paper on for a little longer, and place the container in a slightly brighter position. Gradually acclimatize the seedlings as they develop, giving more light and always ensuring plenty of air, but without draughts. Keep the compost just moist, not wet, and maintain at the same temperature as for germination. Feeding every two weeks or so is advisable to strengthen the seedlings.

Seeds are best sown early in the year, allowing them several months to progress before it becomes necessary to provide a period of dormancy. The seedlings benefit from being left undisturbed for at least six months, or even longer, and should only be pricked out after dormancy, at the start of the growing season. Plants will usually flower after the second year, although this depends on the species concerned.

CUTTINGS AND OFFSETS

Many succulents can be multiplied by leaf cuttings, particularly members of the family Crassulaceae. Carefully remove a leaf from the stem and allow the cut area to dry off. This drying process, which allows a callus or seal to form, is important with all cuttings and may take two or three days. Then insert the base of the leaf into a fine gritty compost so that it is just supported, using a small thin stick if necessary to hold it. Keep the cutting barely moist, well shaded and in a temperature of 70°F (21°C). Rooting may occur in a couple of weeks, but often takes longer. Do not disturb the cutting until it is well established and actively growing.

Stem cuttings can be treated in much the same way. Make the cutting just below a node or leaf axil of the stem, allow the cut section to dry, then insert it in a sandy compost and firm the compost around the node, supporting if necessary. With most succulents, for example, the Euphorbiaceae, Asclepiadaceae and certain other families, a cutting can be taken off a branch where it joins the stem. Give time for the cutting to dry before proceeding as for a stem cutting.

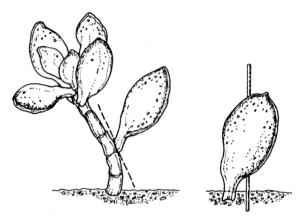

Leaf cutting of a *Crassula* – taking the cutting (left) and inserting it (right)

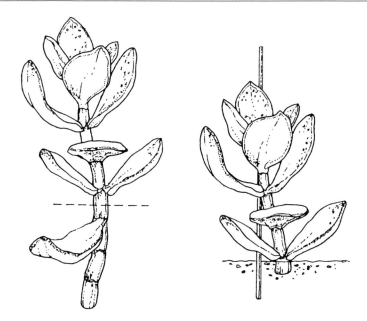

Stem cutting of a *Crassula* – taking the cutting (left) and inserting it (right)

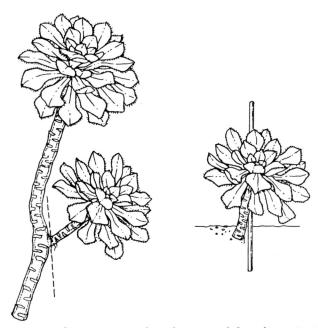

Side stem cutting of an *Aeonium* – taking the cutting (left) and inserting it (right)

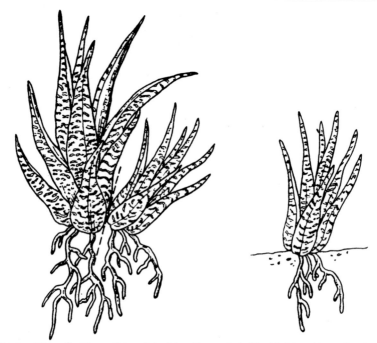

Root cutting of a *Haworthia* – detaching the rooted offset (left) and inserting it (right)

Root cutting of *Ceropegia woodii* – detaching the caudex (above) and inserting it (below)

Ceropegia woodii can be propagated from the rounded tuberous rootstock

Offsets are common in a great number of species. In many instances, they have roots already attached and can be removed from the parent, potted separately and grown on as mature plants. Those without apparent roots should be dealt with in the same way as stem cuttings.

Succulents with a tuberous or stoloniferous rootstock, such as *Ceropegia*, *Aloe* and *Sansevieria*, provide another method of propagation. Sever a tuber or a section of the stolon, first ensuring that it possesses a growing point. Always allow the cut piece to dry, otherwise it might rot when planted. Plant in extra gritty compost, keep at a temperature of 70°F (21°C) and, once new growth becomes evident, grow on in the normal conditions for an established plant.

Cuttings should only be taken during the growing period, using healthy parts of the plant. Make sure that the knife is really sharp and clean. It is a wise precaution against disease to dust the cut with a fungicidal powder.

—— Directory of Succulent Plants ——

It would be impossible to encompass all succulents within the scope of this book and it is therefore confined to the better-known families and the genera and species contained therein, all of which are fairly freely available. Most will undoubtedly be familiar to succulent plant enthusiasts, although a few less common species have been included, in the hope of encouraging collectors to seek out the unusual. None of the plants described can be considered difficult to grow, especially if the general guidelines on cultivation are followed (see pp.80–81). Many are excellent plants for beginners, being both easily cultivated and readily obtainable, and these are indicated in the directory with an asterisk (*). Any particular demands of a genus or species will, of course, be explained where appropriate.

A NOTE ON CLASSIFICATION

In this directory the plants are grouped in families, which are given in alphabetical order, starting with Agavaceae and ending with Vitaceae.

For those unfamiliar with the terminology, a plant family is an assembly of genera sharing certain botanical characteristics; the cactus family, for instance, consists of over 100 genera, all distinguished by the possession of an areole or special growing point. Family names (with only three exceptions) end in '-aceae', as in Crassulaceae, Liliaceae and so on. Each genus (plural – genera) within a family groups together species that have a peculiar affinity with each other, even though they may differ greatly in appearance; thus the spurges, members of the genus *Euphorbia*, all contain a milky sap. Finally, each species within a genus takes the generic name, rather like a surname, followed by its own specific name, like a 'given' name or Christian name, which often conveys its characteristics or origin; *Euphorbia canariensis*, for example, is native to the Canary Islands.

AGAVACEAE

This is an important family of rosette-forming plants of relatively easy culture. Some become very large and can quickly outgrow

Agave americana var. *marginata* has become naturalized along the Mediterranean coast

their alloted space in the greenhouse or home, so careful selection is necessary. Several are hardy and these will be noted. A really open, porous compost is important. Water moderately throughout the growing season. A temperature of 50°F (10°C) is sufficient for all those described below. They are summer-flowering. Propagation is from offsets or seed. (A reclassification has placed *Dracaena* and *Sanseveria* in the new family Dracaenaceae.)

Agave americana, the century plant, is probably native to Mexico, which is the centre of population for this American genus, and has become naturalized in many parts of the world. It has thick, outspreading, glaucous green, spiny edged leaves, which can attain 6½ ft (2 m) in length, each with a prominent spine at the end. The spikes of yellowish green flowers appear only when the plant is large and mature, reaching 20 ft (6 m) or more in sub-tropical regions, after which the main rosette dies (a feature of all agaves). It should be noted that this species becomes very big with age and could be an embarrassment in the average greenhouse. However, it can be planted outdoors in a protected spot, especially in southern Britain. Popular varieties include *mediopicta*, with a wide yellow stripe down the centre of the greyish green leaves; *mediopicta* forma *alba*, which has a white band in the middle and in generally a more compact, smaller plant; and the well-known *marginata*,* with yellow margins to the greenish leaves.
A. filifera is a large widespreading rosette up to about 20 in. (50 cm) high. The dark green leaves have white markings and numerous curved, whitish threads at the edges. The flowers are greenish purple or yellowish green with long stamens.
A. stricta has many slender, stiff, tapering leaves some 1 ft (30 cm) long, which form a neat, dense, erect rosette. The flowers are borne on a 6½ ft (2 m) stem.

91

Calibanus hookeri, a curious plant with a distinctive caudex, which is its main attraction

A. utahensis, a native of mountainous areas of the USA, has several varieties. They are low plants rarely exceeding 1 ft (30 cm) across, with greyish green, spiny edged leaves. Particularly attractive is the variety *eborispina*, which has more greyish leaves, each with a long greyish white terminal spine.

A. victoriae-reginae is one of the finest agaves. The dense rosette is made up of incurved, dark green, white-patterned leaves, distinctly ridged on the under-surface and up to 6 in. (15 cm) long. There are a number of varieties (see p. 72).

Calibanus hookeri comes from Mexico, where it is scarcely distinguishable from the surrounding grassland. It is an interesting caudiciform plant, with a large caudex reaching 1 ft (30 cm) or more in diameter and covered in a corky bark. In cultivation the caudex is visible above the compost and from it sprout long, coarse, tough, grass-like leaves. The inconspicuous flowers are pinkish purple.

Dracaena draco is native to the Canary Islands and representative of a few members of this genus which are truly succulent. The sword-shaped leaves are glaucous green and reddish at the base, forming loose rosettes at the tips of the branches. The dragon tree, as it is called, is said to live to a great age and can be easily grown from seed, flowering after only a few years. It is an excellent houseplant.

Sansevieria cylindrica originates from west Africa and has completely cylindrical, deep green leaves tapering to a hard tip. The white flowers are produced on a tall spike 3 ft (90 cm) high.

An example of *Dracaena draco* growing in Tenerife; it is reputed to be 1,000 years old

S. trifasciata, also from west Africa, has a rhizomatous rootstock and each shoot carries about six stiff, flat, leaves banded with pale greenish lines. The variety *laurentii*,* which is a popular houseplant, has leaves with white or yellow stripes along the edges (see p. 120).

Yucca baccata from Arizona and California has a stiff erect rosette of leaves about 3 ft (90 cm) long, edged with whitish fibres and a terminal spine. The flowers are white. Like many yuccas, it is almost hardy and flourishes outside in the mild southwest of Britain.

Y. brevifolia, the Joshua tree, is widely distributed in the southern USA and northern Mexico. It develops a long trunk with a number of branches, each ending in a smallish rosette of narrow leaves.

Y. texanum from Texas has very slender, greyish green leaves with long thread-like hairs along their length. The flower spike, over $3\frac{1}{4}$ ft (1 m) high, bears large lily-like flowers and the rootstock is slightly tuberous and stoloniferous. It is a most attractive plant, but somewhat uncommon.

APOCYNACEAE

This family includes many succulent species from both the Old and New World. They have considerable appeal for enthusiasts,

93

especially those plants with a caudex. The majority are tropical and consequently require greater care in cultivation, although several make good houseplants. A rich porous compost is essential, together with regular feeding and careful watering during the growing season. A minimum temperature of 61°F (16°C) is advisable, even during the dormant period. They flower in summer. Propagation is usually by seed.

Adenium obesum is found in many parts of Africa and in Saudi Arabia, with several localized varieties. It has a thick fleshy caudex, often like a stout bottle-shaped trunk, which in maturity can reach 3¼ ft (1 m) or more tall. It is sometimes branching, with glossy green, oval leaves spirally arranged at the tips. The flowers give ample justification for the common name of desert rose: they are large pink to carmine-rose and more or less funnel-shaped with wide-spreading petals. It is easily raised from seed, flowering when quite young.

Pachypodium geayi reaches about 25 ft (7.5 m) high in its native Madagascar and has slender palm-like leaves about 16 in. (40 cm) long, the undersurfaces covered in minute grey hairs. Quite small plants are sometimes offered, which are ideal for indoors, but the cream-coloured flowers appear only on very mature specimens.

P. lamerei,* known as the Madagascan palm, can grow to 20 ft (6 m) high, the base of the caudex being about 2 ft (60 cm) in diameter and tending to branch from near the top. The leaves are up to 16 in. (40 cm) long, while the white flowers are about 2 in. (5 cm) across and borne on a long slender tube. Small plants are becoming available as houseplants.

P. namaquanum is a South African species with a long, fleshy, thick, thorny trunk or caudex, eventually up to 6½ ft (2 m) tall. The short hairy leaves, with wavy edges, are produced in tufts from the top of the trunk and maroon-red yellow-striped flowers appear from the leaf axils.

P. rosulatum is native to Madagascar and varies according to its different environments. The variety gracilis is a slender plant with a rounded fleshy caudex, a few small terminal leaves and deep yellow flowers (see p. 78).

Plumiera acuminata,* the frangipani tree from Central and South America, has a succulent fleshy stem and branches which exude a type of latex if punctured. The large oblong leaves are shed during dormancy, after which the beautiful flowers are produced, highly scented and dark cream with a yellow centre. The variety rubra is similar to the type, but has lovely carmine-red flowers with a yellow centre.

ASCLEPIADACEAE

This family contains some of the most fascinating succulents, often with extraordinary flowers, which are produced in late spring or summer. Many are low-growing, coming from semi-arid areas, while others inhabit forests, a number even being epiphytic or tree-dwelling. Unless otherwise stated, all the plants described need a bright position, although not necessarily in full sun, an open compost, very careful watering, keeping them almost dry during the rest season, and a minimum temperature of 61°F (16°C). Propagation is normally easy from seed.

Left: The frangipani tree, *Plumiera acuminata*, is widely grown throughout the tropics for its fragrant flowers
Right: Unlike most other Asclepiadaceae, *Ceropegia haygarthii* should have a partly shaded position

---

Caralluma europaea is from southern Spain and North Africa. The branching often prostrate stems are four-angled and greyish green with reddish markings. The flowers are greenish yellow with brown lines, carried in umbels of about ten. There are several varieties, the flowers sometimes more purplish or green with reddish marks in the centre or, in the case of the variety *simonis*, reddish brown with numerous white and brownish hairs.

C. joannis is a well-known species from Morocco, similar to *C. europaea*, except that the stems are wavy edged and finely toothed. The flowers, in clusters, are greenish yellow with reddish spots on the tube and velvety purple, brownish lobes.

C. plicatiloba is a free-branching species from Yemen and Saudi Arabia. The erect, bluish green stems are four-angled with rounded teeth. The flowers, borne in racemes, are yellowish with reddish brown markings, the edges whitish and densely covered in purple-tipped hairs.

Ceropegia dichotoma from the Canary Islands is upright, up to 2 ft (60 cm) or more tall. The stems are greyish green and the flowers yellow with a curved tube.

C. haygarthii (*C. distincta* subsp. *haygarthii*) is a native of South Africa, in particular Natal. It is a twinning plant with succulent stems and small oval leaves. The slender funnel-shaped flowers have a slightly curved tube and are creamy coloured with maroon flecks and dots and a maroon interior, from the centre of which arises a thin maroon 'stalk' topped with a reddish purple knob with a few whitish hairs. A semi-shaded position is necessary.

*C. woodii** is sometimes called the string of hearts on account of the small heart-shaped leaves set in pairs along the wiry trailing branches. The leaves are bluish green marbled with silver and purplish on the undersides, while the tiny flowers are purplish brown with a fringe of purple hairs. It comes from South Africa and has a rounded tuberous rootstock. This is a popular houseplant and looks attractive in a hanging basket. Partial shade is advisable (see p. 89).

Diplocyatha see *Orbea*.

Duvalia pillansii form the Karroo, South Africa, has numerous thick, greenish reddish stems, which are four-angled with a few teeth along the edges and about 1 in. (2.5 cm) long. The freely produced flowers have triangular lobes, purplish brown on the upper surface, greenish below, and are pale yellowish in the middle, with a fleshy central ring which is first whitish becoming purplish.

Left: The flowers of *Duvalia sulcata* have the fleshy central disk characteristic of the genus
Right: Species of *Hoodia*, such as *H. gordonii*, have relatively large flowers

---

D. sulcata is a small prostrate species from Arabia, with pale greyish green, purple-spotted stems, four-angled and prominently toothed. The flowers are brownish red and the glossy central ring is densely covered with reddish hairs.

Hoodia bainii from Cape Province, South Africa, through to Namibia, is often confused with *H. gordonii*, but lacks the small nipples in the centre of the yellowish pinkish flowers. It is a bushy plant about 8 in. (20 cm) high and has cylindrical stems with many longitudinal ribs and tubercles armed with spined tips.

H. gordonii from Namibia is up to 18 in. (45 cm) tall. The stems have regular rib-like angles along their length, which carry protuberances with woody spines. The large, almost circular flowers are pale purplish with dark reddish nipples in the centre, but are not readily produced in cultivation.

Hoya australis, an Australian species, is a climber with thick fleshy leaves of dark green, sometimes speckled whitish. The flowers, in umbels, are waxy white with a reddish centre. This is an epiphyte, requiring semi-shade and reasonable humidity, and the compost should never be allowed to dry out completely.

H. bella (*H. lanceolata* subsp. *bella*)* is a native of Burma and familiar as a houseplant. The arching stems bear small fleshy leaves and umbels consisting of eight or nine sweetly scented, waxy white flowers with rose-pink centres. It is a true epiphyte which can be grown to perfection in a hanging basket.

H. carnosa* is another well-known species, a vigorous climber originating from China and Australia. The leaves are oval, thick and fleshy and the flowers are gathered in large, often dense umbels, being pinkish white with a red centre and fragrant. Semi-shade is advisable and it is an excellent plant for the home (see p.124).

H. linearis is a sub-tropical epiphyte from the Himalayas. The stems and branches are very soft, slender, greyish green and pendulous, while the narrow, almost cylindrical leaves are hairy and dark green. Small, pure white flowers are borne in drooping clusters. Shade and a minimum temperature of 61°F (16°C) are essential for this species and it should be sprayed regularly in warm weather, never allowing the compost to dry out completely. It is ideal for a hanging basket.

H. purpurea-fusca from the forests of Java is a clambering or trailing plant to 13 ft (4 m) in length. The dark green leaves are often flecked with silver and the flowers, in large umbels, are reddish purple or purplish brown. A shaded position is imperative and the compost should always be slightly moist.

Left: The flowers of *Hoya australis* are scented of honeysuckle
Right: The ten-pointed flower of *Huernia striata*, with shorter points between
the main lobes, is typical of the genus

Huernia oculata from Namibia produces many reddish green stems about 4 in.
(10 cm) long, five-angled and with fleshy teeth. Flowers appear from the base of the
new growth and have five large and five very small lobes of dark, almost blackish red
and a pure white centre.

H. schneiderana from Malawi and Mozambique has stems up to 8 in. (20 cm) long,
with toothed angles. The bell-shaped flower is brownish on the outer surface and
velvety, deep purple inside, the margins pinkish and edged with maroon.

H. striata has bluntly angled stems up to 3 in. (8 cm) high. The flowers are about 1 in.
(2.5 cm) across, the tube greenish or maroon on the outside, yellow inside, the lobes
also yellow and the whole marked with irregular, brownish maroon bands.

Luckhoffia beukmanii from Cape Province, South Africa, grows about 28 in. (70 cm)
tall. The slightly hairy, greyish green stems have nine angles raised in tubercles. The
large flowers, two or three together, are brownish with yellow dots or maroon red
with minute yellowish spots (see p. 74).

Orbea ciliata (*Diplocyatha ciliata*) from the Karroo, South Africa, has four-angled,
prominently toothed stems about 2 in. (5 cm) long. The whitish flowers, borne
singly, are about 3 in. (8 cm) across; the edges of the spreading lobes are hairy and
the funnel-shaped central ring has a recurved rim and is dotted with purple.

O. semota (*Stapelia semota*) from Kenya and Tanzania has stems up to 3 in. (8 cm) tall,
smooth and four-angled with spreading teeth. The flowers have deep brownish
lobes with paler markings and a dark brown five-angled ring edged with reddish
hairs.

O. variegata (*Stapelia variegata*)* is one of the commonest of this group with
beautiful, but evil-smelling flowers. The stems are about 4 in. (10 cm) high, bluntly
angled, greyish green and with projecting teeth. The starfish-like flowers vary
according to the variety, of which there are many. In the variety *atropurpurea*,
which is very much like the species, the flower is about 3 in. (8 cm) across and the
lobes have a wrinkled surface, the tips being yellow with dark brownish purple
marks and the centre blackish purple with a few circular markings. It is from Cape
Province, South Africa (see p. 124).

Stapelia erectiflora has slender downy stems about 6 in. (15 cm) high. The flowers are
a particular feature: carried on long stalks, they are greyish purple densely covered
with white hairs, only about $\frac{1}{2}$ in. (1 cm) across and with the lobes rolled right back,

Left: The striking five-lobed flower of *Tridentea longipes*
Right: A member of the Commelinaceae, *Tripogandra warscewicziana* needs a
semi-shaded position

giving a rounded effect like a Turkish fez. Southern and central Africa is the home of
the genus.

S. flavopurpurea has bluish green, four-angled stems some 2 in. (5 cm) tall. The small
flowers are more or less flat and have five lobes covered with minute, purplish red
wrinkles and a central white disc with many pinkish red hairs.

S. schinzii is another small plant, having four-angled, dark green, purple-mottled
stems. The large flower, about 5 in. (12 cm) in diameter, has five elongated, tapering
lobes, blackish purple, wrinkled and edged with purple hairs. It is a variable species,
depending on the habitat.

Trichocaulon pedicellatum from the Namib desert of southwest Africa is one of the
smallest members of this genus. It has cylindrical ridged stems and dark reddish
brown flowers with tapering lobes, borne on short stalks from the sides of the stems.

T. pillansii from Cape Province, South Africa, can attain 7 in. (18 cm) in height. The
greyish green stems have warts with bristly tips, while the bright yellow flowers
have pinkish nipples just discernible on the margins.

Tridentea longipes (*Stapelia longipes*) comes from Namibia and is a low cushion-
forming plant with smooth, bluish green stems. The purplish flowers, about 2 in.
(5 cm) across, have lobes widening towards the centre, then tapering to the tips, with
a wrinkled surface; they are blotched and lined with white near the throat and
fringed at the edges.

COMMELINACEAE

This family contains several species which are truly succulent in
stem or leaf, many of them trailing or creeping, and make ideal
houseplants. A semi-shady position and fairly rich, open compost
are advisable and they should be watered freely during the growing
season but, in the case of the deciduous species, kept reasonably
dry until new growth develops. The flowers appear in summer.
They are easily propagated from cuttings or seeds.

Cyanotis lanata is a densely leaved plant from tropical Africa, with stems about 1 ft (30 cm) long and a cottony hairy appearance. The flowers, mainly purple or pink, are clustered in the upper axils of the stems. It needs plenty of moisture.
C. somaliensis, a native of Somalia and neighbouring countries, is similar. The stems and leaves are white-furry and very fleshy and the flowers blue. It is deciduous.
*Tradescantia navicularis** from Peru is possibly the most succulent member of this genus, which includes the well-known trailing houseplants called Wandering Jew. The short-jointed creeping stems root at the nodes and form mats. The small boat-shaped leaves are fleshy, greyish green and minutely fringed and the flowers are purplish pink.
T. sillamontana is a deciduous species from northern Mexico. The stems are white, hairy, about 2 in. (5 cm) or more long and densely clothed with thick green leaves, coated with fine white hairs. The flowers vary from pink to mauve.
Tripogandra warscewicziana is native to Guatemala. The thick succulent stems develop a rosette of dark green, slightly recurved leaves and the long-lasting flowers of deep purple are borne in clusters on a branched head. This is a splendid plant for the home or greenhouse.

COMPOSITAE (ASTERACEAE)

The daisy family is one of the largest in the plant kingdom and embraces a great number of true succulents of all kinds – stem, leaf, root, even caudiciform. Most have the typical daisy flowers, consisting of numerous disc or ray florets densely set together and surrounded by colourful or greenish bracts. These are produced in summer. The majority are of easy culture, given a sunny position, and should be watered freely in the growing season and kept fairly dry during the remainder of the year. A temperature of 50°F (10°C) is sufficient, unless otherwise stated. Propagation is best by cuttings.

Coreopsis gigantea is a robust fleshy plant up to 6½ ft (2 m) high. It is surmounted by a thick tuft of feathery leaves and a cluster of pale yellowish flowers, each about 3 in. (8 cm) across. It should be allowed to rest in the warmest months and be kept reasonably dry, then encouraged into growth as cooler weather arrives.
Kleinia fulgens (*Senecio fulgens*) from Natal is a tuberous-rooted plant with prostrate stems up to 18 in. (45 cm) long. These are pale grey and powdery, as are the pale green leaves, while the small flower heads are reddish.
K. galpinii (*Senecio galpinii*) grows about 2 ft (60 cm) tall, with pale greyish stems and leaves and three to four flower heads bearing pale orange-red blooms. It comes from the Transvaal.
Othonna pygmaea is a dwarf South African species. It has almost a caudex base, a very short stem bearing broad fleshy leaves, which are deciduous, and yellow flowers at the top.
O. sedifolia from Namibia is a bushy plant about 2 ft (60 cm) high and across, with thick robust stems. The somewhat cylindrical leaves are spirally arranged at the tips of the shoots and have prominent tubercles on the upper surface. The flower head has bright yellow ray florets.
*Senecio articulatus** is almost 2 ft (60 cm) high, the cylindrical stem being a series of swollen joints, greyish green with purplish markings, which are its outstanding

feature. The flowers are yellowish. It is found in southern Africa, like the other species described here.

S. haworthii grows up to 12 in. (30 cm) high. The cylindrical pointed leaves and the stems are coated with a white felt. The yellow flowers are arranged in a large head, but not always produced in cultivation.

S. rowleyanus* has many creeping slender stems, bearing numerous, almost spherical, tiny leaves. It is known as the string of beads. The flowers are insignificant but cinnamon-scented.

S. stapeliiformis is an erect species, with branching angular stems. The new shoots commence underground before emerging and are purplish brown and grey with dark green markings and lines, set at intervals with small leaves, which quickly wither. The flowers, on a long stalk, are bright red.

CONVOLVULACEAE

This is a large family involving many genera and species, which are worldwide in distribution. Some are shrubs, others, like the well-known convolvulus and morning glory, are climbing or trailing and a few are even parasitic. A comparatively small number can justifiably be termed succulents and these have a thick tuberous or caudiciform rootstock. While in nature the caudex is invariably underground, in cultivation it has been found advisable to leave it exposed, with just the base anchored in the compost. Water well once new growth becomes evident and then, after the leaves and flowers have died down, withhold water until the following season. The plants flower from mid- to late summer. Temperatures may soar while they are in growth and a minimum of 50°F (10°C) is recommended when they are resting. They should be partially shaded. Propagation is by seed.

Ipomoea batatas is apparently of Indian origin, but is widely grown in tropical and sub-tropical regions for the tuberous root, which is the edible sweet potato. The prostrate, slightly fleshy stems have roughly triangular leaves up to 5½ in. (14 cm) long, either entire or with three to five lobes. The flowers are pinkish white.

I. bolusii, a South African species, has a large rounded caudex with a greyish bark. It is a deciduous plant and the grass-like leaves rise directly from the crown of the caudex or sometimes on a short stem. The flowers are funnel-shaped, pinkish lilac and usually larger than the caudex.

I. inamoena from Namibia has a large caudex 6 in. (15 cm) or more wide, with a brownish or almost black skin. The stems are about 20 in. (50 cm) long, either prostrate or semi-erect, with thick elongated leaves, fringed on the margins. Large funnel-shaped flowers of lilac to pale pink appear from the leaf axils.

Turbina holubii from the Transvaal has a large brownish caudex, from which develops a short stem with very slender, long, deciduous leaves. The purplish pink flowers are bell-shaped, opening widely at the tips.

CRASSULACEAE

This is one of the larger families of succulent plants. In general they are of easy culture and some, such as Sedum, Sempervivum and

Left: *Senecio haworthii* is noticeable for the pure white woolly covering on stems and leaves
Right: The lovely flowers of *Turbina holubii* have a resemblance to those of convolvulus

---

certain *Echeveria* species, are even hardy if planted outdoors in very porous soil. There are very few problems with species from Europe, although those of tropical or sub-tropical origin should have a minimum temperature of 50°F (10°C) and need to be kept reasonably dry during the rest period. For most, a porous compost is advised and the containers should afford ample space for plants of trailing or spreading habit. The flowering time is spring to late summer. Propagation is by stem cuttings, offsets or seed.

Adromischus festivus (*A. cooperi*) from Cape Province, South Africa, has a very short stem carrying cylindrical or thick wedge-shaped leaves, often with wavy margins and with the lower surface much rounded, of silvery green marbled with maroon. The insignificant flowers are borne on a 10 in. (25 cm) long stem.
A. mammillaris has bluish green, waxy, spindle-shaped leaves and greenish brown flowers in summer.
Aeonium arboreum from the southern Mediterranean region grows about 3¼ ft (1 m) high, with rosettes of green leaves, 8 in. (3 cm) across, at the tips of the erect stems. The variety *atropurpurea*,* when placed in full sun, has blackish red leaves and is a splendid plant for a sunny windowsill (see p. 102).
A. nobile is found in the Canary Islands, where most other members of the genus are concentrated. It has a short-stemmed rosette about 20 in. (50 cm) across, each long, light green, sticky leaf being very succulent, with curved margins. The leafy flower head is about 20 in. (50 cm) tall, with brownish red flowers in spring, although these are not produced until the plant is some seven years old.
A. smithii has very hairy stems and branches carrying an open rosette about 4 in. (10 cm) across. The leaves are yellowish green with reddish lines along them and wavy edges and the flowers are pale yellow in early spring.
A. tabuliforme* grows almost flattened to the rock-face in the Canary Islands. It is a completely rounded, flat rosette about 20 in. (50 cm) across, consisting of bright

Aeonium arboreum, from Morocco, is a familiar sight in Mediterranean countries, where it has become widely naturalized

green leaves, with fine hairs on the edges. Deep yellow flowers are borne on a branched head up to 2 ft (60 cm) high in spring. It offsets freely.

Cotyledon ladismithensis comes from South Africa, as do the other species mentioned here. It is a choice bushy plant up to 12 in. (30 cm) tall. The fleshy, hairy, oblong leaves are set in four opposite pairs. The flower head bears shiny yellow flowers tinged with deep orange in summer.

C. orbiculata grows over 3¼ ft (1 m) tall, with very thick, fleshy stems, freely branching. The thick oval leaves are covered entirely with a waxy white frosting and the summer flowers are yellowish red. The variety *ausana* is similar, except that the leaves have a reddish margin.

C. undulata* is a popular species, growing over 20 in. (50 cm) tall. The broad opposite leaves are coated with a silvery grey bloom and have prominently wavy margins towards the tips. A tall stem bears several nodding orange-red flowers in summer.

Crassula argentea* (*C. ovata*) is native to southern Africa, as are the majority of the species. A tree-like plant which in the wild can attain well over 3¼ ft (1 m) in height, it has a thick fleshy stem and branches with fleshy, dark green leaves, often spotted with slightly darker green. White or pinkish white flowers are produced in profusion in late winter and early spring. It is of easy culture and excellent for the home.

C. barbata, by contrast, forms a compact, basal rosette only 1½ in. (3–4 cm) across, of incurved, dull green leaves edged with numerous projecting hairs. The flowers are small and whitish, in late spring.

C. lactea is a low, bushy plant, with erect or semi-prostrate branches. The flattish, fleshy, long-pointed leaves are green with whitish dots, while the white scented flowers are borne in dense clusters at the ends of the stalks in early summer.

C. multicava is a freely branching species about 12 in. (30 cm) tall. The leaves may be greyish or glossy green, minutely spotted, about as long as wide. The pinkish white flowers are very small but produced in great numbers on long, curved, slender stems in summer.

C. perforata is a small shrub-like plant with woody stems and branches. The broad, greyish green leaves have many red spots, particularly near the edges, and the rather small flowers are bright yellow, appearing in early summer. The paramount feature is the chain-like effect created by the arrangement of the leaves, which seem to completely surround the slender branches.

C. rosularis has a basal rosette of many dark, glossy green leaves which taper to a point, about 3 in. (8 cm) long. The rosette produces offsets, making quite dense groups. In late spring, numerous clusters of small white flowers are carried at the ends of long stalks, which tend to branch.

C. teres is a clump-forming plant with short stems and densely compacted leaves in four rows, making short leafy columns. The leaves have transparent margins and the flowers are white, in early summer.

Dudleya farinosa, from the coast of northern California, has a short branching stem, from the tips of which develop green or white-powdered leafy rosettes up to 4 in. (10 cm) across. The branched flower head is about 12 in. (30 cm) tall, with pale yellow flowers in summer.

Echeveria derenbergii,* a popular and well-known species, comes from Mexico, as do the other echeverias described here. It forms dense cushions of roughly cylindrical rosettes about $2\frac{1}{2}$ in. (6 cm) across. The leaves are waxy white on pale green and red-tipped, the margins also being reddish. The flowers are reddish yellow, in late spring.

E. lilacina is one of the more recent introductions. Plants have short thick stems with a rosette some 6 in. (15 cm) across, consisting of brownish green leaves covered with pinkish white wax-like powder. Clusters of drooping, pinkish orange flowers are borne at the ends of long slender stems in early summer.

E. nodulosa has stems and leaves densely covered with minute nipples. It is a prostrate species with slow-growing elongated stems and branches and sometimes aerial roots. The reddish-marked leaves form a dense rosette about 5 in. (13 cm) across. The flowers are yellow with a red base, borne on a stem up to 2 ft (60 cm) long in early summer.

E. pulvinata has a lax rosette of oval leaves about 2 in. (5 cm) long, very thick and fleshy and covered with whitish hairs. The reddish flowers have prominent yellow stamens and are carried on a leafy, horizontally spreading, hairy stem in summer.

E. setosa* has a stemless rosette of closely set, dark greenish leaves covered with minute white bristles. The reddish yellow flowers are borne at the top of a 12 in. (30 cm) stem and produced from midsummer to early autumn. This has played a part in some of the Echeveria hybrids which have been produced, but none can surpass the species themselves (see p. 104).

Graptopetalum bellum (Tacitus bellus)* won the admiration of plant enthusiasts when it was discovered in 1972 in the mountains of northern Mexico. It has a neat fleshy rosette about 2 in. (5 cm) in diameter and bright red star-like flowers on short stems in summer (see p. 84).

G. macdougallii, also from Mexico, is a dwarf species with a short stem and produces several offsets, each having an individual rosette of bluish leaves. The flowers are greenish white with reddish tips to the petals, appearing in late spring and early summer.

Kalanchoe beharensis is probably the tallest species in the genus, able to attain 10 ft (3 m) in height. The arrow-shaped leaves have a very fleshy blade and are up to 8 in.

Left: *Echeveria setosa* is easy to grow and makes offsets freely
Right: *Kalanchoe tomentosa* seldom flowers in cultivation but is attractive for its woolly covering

---

(20 cm) long, olive-green with greyish waxy covering and heavily toothed at the edges. The flower head is about 2 ft (60 cm) high and has small, insignificant, whitish flowers in late summer. It is native to Madagascar, along with the majority of species under consideration.

K. blossfeldiana* is a popular houseplant which has been hybridized to make many different flower colours available, from yellow to orange and pinkish to deep scarlet. Growing about 12 in. (30 cm) high, it has oblong leaves of dark glossy green, often reddish and notched at the margins. The heads of small flowers are normally reddish and produced in summer. The hybrids offered at Christmas time are mainly forced for winter flowering and are best treated as annuals. However, cuttings can be taken in early spring from those which have survived the winter (see p. 83).

K. fedtschenkoi is also popular in cultivation. The leaves are bluish green, fleshy and oblong, with the edges toothed towards the base, and the flowers are pinkish, in summer.

K. manganii,* also low-growing, has woody stems and numerous branches clad in very succulent, tiny leaves, sometimes minutely hairy. Reddish flowers hang from the spreading branches in late spring. It is an excellent houseplant.

K. marmorata from Somalia, Sudan and Kenya is usually an upright plant branching from the base. The oval leaves, about 4 in. (10 cm) long, are greyish green marbled with brownish blotches and have toothed margins. The flowers are whitish, in early summer.

K. pumila* is semi-pendent with stems and branches 8–10 in. (20–25 cm) long. The greyish green leaves are stalkless and partly notched at the edges, while the flowers are slightly drooping, urn-shaped and reddish violet, in small panicles, in late spring.

K. tomentosa* is up to 18 in. (45 cm) tall, erect, sometimes branching from the base and thickly white-felted all over. The stalkless leaves are densely set along the branches and tipped with a distinctive brown blotch. The flowers are reddish on a tall stem, in summer.

K. tubiflora* is probably the best-known member of the genus. Growing up to 3½ ft (1 cm) high, it is very fleshy and produces a tall compact head of reddish purple, bell-shaped blooms in summer.

Pachyphytum oviferum* from Mexico has a short, thick, fleshy, white stem, with

104

Left: The sugar-almond plant, *Pachyphytum oviferum*, has a dense white coating
Right: The well-known ice plant, *Sedum spectabile*, is perfectly hardy in Britain

terminal, very succulent, oval leaves, finely powdered in white or pinkish; the leaf shape and colour have won it the common name of sugar-almond plant. The bell-shaped flowers are greenish white with a reddish centre, ten or more on a delicately curved spike, appearing in early summer.

P. viride has small, greenish purplish leaves which are semi-cylindrical, especially near the base, borne on a thick, fleshy, brownish stem about 4 in. (10 cm) high. The reddish green flowers are carried in a panicle.

Sedum adolphii originates from Mexico, as do the next two species. It is fairly bushy, with thick fleshy branches and small reddish yellow leaves. The flowers are white, in early summer.

S. frutescens is up to 32 in. (80 cm) tall and the very fleshy stem is covered with a papery bark, giving it some resemblance to a bonsai tree. The narrow leaves are edged with minute warts and the flowers are white, in early summer.

S. hintonii has a compact dense rosette of oblong, fleshy, glaucous green leaves, so densely hairy as to appear whitish. The star-like flowers are green and white with prominent reddish anthers, produced in early spring.

S. montanum is a hardy species from the European Pyrenees, which forms a thick cushion of creeping shoots and narrow, dark green or reddish leaves. It does not exceed 6 in. (15 cm), even when the golden yellow flowers are produced in summer.

S. palmeri* from Mexico has stem and basal rosettes of broad, bluish green leaves. The star-like golden yellow flowers are borne at the end of branched heads in early spring.

S. praealtum from Mexico and Guatemala is a tall species which develops shrub-like proportions. Several stout fleshy stems over 2 ft (60 cm) high arise from the base, bearing fleshy green leaves up to 2 in. (5 cm) long and topped by panicles of bright yellow flowers in late spring and early summer. It is reasonably hardy in southern Britain.

S. sieboldii* is the well-known hardy species from Japan. The stems are up to 9 in. (25 cm) long, reddish and prostrate, while the leaves are bluish grey, rounded and arranged in whorls of three. The flowers are pink, in late summer. The variegated form, with yellowish white blotches on the foliage, is equally popular.

S. spectabile* from China is another familiar garden plant, often called the ice plant. It has fleshy roots, stems and leaves and is deciduous. Erect-growing up to 9 in.

(25 cm) tall, it has oval leaves, often with toothed margins, of light waxy green. The almost flat flower head consists of many pale pink blooms in late summer. There are several interesting cultivars, such as 'Ruby Glow', with reddish leaves and red flowers, and 'Variegatum', with pale green leaves mottled yellowish white and deep pink flowers (see p.105).

*Sempervivum arachnoideum,** the cobweb houseleek, is a mountain plant of Europe and completely hardy in Britain. The small rosettes of green leaves are covered with densely tangled, white, cobweb-like hairs. The flowers are usually reddish, although a white form is known.

S. tectorum is a European native. The greenish leaves, sometimes tipped with reddish brown and whitish towards the base, form a rosette up to 5½ in. (14 cm) across. In general, the flowers are pinkish or red, in summer, although there are many varieties differing in leaf and flower colour. It is hardy.

Tacitus see *Graptopetalum*.

CUCURBITACEAE

The cucumber family includes many genera from both the Old and New World. Most are annual, but it is those succulent species whose rootstock develops a caudex that capture the imagination of plant enthusiasts. Although these are perhaps more for the advanced collector, it must be stressed that they present very little difficulty in cultivation. The essential requirement is really open compost, for in the main the caudex rests on the soil surface with the base just below, so that only the roots penetrate the compost and anchor the plant firmly. A dry resting period is imperative. They flower in summer. Propagation is from seed.

Gerrardanthus macrorhizus is a sturdy climbing species from southern and eastern Africa. It has a huge boulder-like caudex, often 2 ft (60 cm) or more across, but can be grown in a pot for several years until the size of caudex makes this impossible. The stems are semi-succulent, with roughly triangular leaves, and the brownish green flowers are followed by yellowish fruits.

Kedrostis africana from Namibia and South Africa has become fairly well known in cultivation. It is a very succulent, fleshy, white caudex which lengthens in maturity. The long stems bear rough triangular leaves about 4 in. (10 cm) long, with toothed margins, and many tendrils to support its growth. The greenish flowers are succeeded by berry-like reddish fruits.

EUPHORBIACEAE

The spurges are one of the largest families and embrace plants from weeds to exotics, including the popular poinsettia, *Euphorbia pulcherrima*. This cosmopolitan group contains many genera and in the region of 5,000 species, some of which resemble cacti. They have one thing in common – a white, often poisonous sap or latex which exudes from a cut or damaged surface. The 'flower' is known as a cyathium and is a combination of often picturesque bracts and small flowers, produced from late spring to midsummer. Careful attention should be given to cultivation. A minimum temperature of 50°F (10°C) is a must, while plants from equatorial regions should be kept even warmer in winter. Water them freely in the growing season, but never allow them to have wet feet or rot can easily set in. Completely dry conditions are necessary throughout dormancy. Propagation is by seed or by cuttings of branching species.

*Euphorbia canariensis** from the Canary Islands is a variable species. The greenish stems are capable of reaching 40 ft (12 m) in the wild and branch from the base. They bear pairs of thorns at intervals along the longitudinal ribs formed by the acute angles.

*E. caput-medusae** has a short caudex bearing numerous branches, spreading almost horizontally to make a flattened rosette-like plant. The whole effect has been likened to a Medusa's head and is enhanced when the many small yellowish cyathia develop at the tips of the young branches. It and the next three species come from Cape Province, South Africa (see p. 108).

E. grandicornis is a clump-forming species with usually three-angled branches, which are irregularly constricted, wavy edged and very thorny. The small orange-yellow cyathia appear towards the ends of the branches. It is a popular and sought-after species of easy culture, but demanding of space since it can grow up to 6 ft (2 m) high in nature.

E. horrida reaches 3 ft (1 m) tall, sometimes with branches from the base. The stems are 4–5 in. (10–13 cm) thick, furrowed lengthwise to form ribs and with toothed thorny angles. The cyathia are yellow.

E. meloformis is a globular plant about 4 in. (10 cm) tall and across, greenish grey and distinctly ribbed, with the angles marked with reddish lines. The cyathium is yellowish.

*E. milii** from Madagascar is the well-known crown of thorns. It is a bushy species with thorny branches and fresh green, oblong to rounded leaves. The cyathia may be red, pink, white, yellow or variegated, depending on the variety (see p. 78)

E. obesa is a desirable species from Cape Province, South Africa, similar to *E. meloformis*, but more rounded and slightly larger. The ribs are set well apart, bearing many reddish lines and striped. It is very reminiscent of certain cacti.

*Jatropha podagrica** from Central America has a thick oblong base to the branched stem. This can reach 3¼ ft (1 m) or more high in its habitat, but is normally much shorter in cultivation – up to 16 in. (40 cm), at which stage the plant is mature and will flower. The three-lobed leaves are about 6 in. (15 cm) long, generally six to eight together at the tips of the branches. The branched flower head carries numerous bright crimson blooms (see p. 108).

Pedilanthus carinatus is a short bushy plant about 18 in. (45 cm) high. The oval leaves are set regularly along the length of the branches and bird-like pinkish and white flowers appear in clusters. It is a native of the West Indies, invariably growing close to the sea (see p. 108).

P. macrocarpus from Mexico has a thick fleshy stem over 3¼ ft (1 m) high, often branching from the base. The oval leaves are small and fleshy and deciduous. The flower head carries a few reddish cyathia, slightly resembling a small bird.

GERANIACEAE

This family contains many popular plants, in particular, the pelargoniums of the window box and the geraniums or cranesbills of the

Above: *Euphorbia caput-medusae* (left) requires a sunny spot or the branches become elongated
Right: *Jatropha podagrica*, a popular houseplant which flowers when young
Below: *Pedilanthus carinatus* (left) belongs to a genus sometimes known as slipper spurge or bird cactus
Right: *Pelargonium barklyi* is recognizable as a member of the Geraniaceae from the flowers

garden. A large number are true succulents, mainly root or stem succulents. They require a minimum temperature of 50°F (10°C) during the winter months, when they must be kept dry. Use an open compost, with good drainage, water freely throughout the growing season and give them good light. They flower in summer. Propagation is from cuttings or seed.

Pelargonium barklyi comes from South Africa, which is the home of nearly all the species. It has a tuberous rootstock, a short stem and many small, heart-shaped leaves near ground level, which are wrinkled with deep-set veins and purplish green. The flowers are borne at the end of a stem about 12 in. (30 cm) long, five to seven in a cluster, and are creamy white veined with deep pink.
P. cotyledonis from the island of St Helena is rarely more than 12 in. (30 cm) tall. It has a thick fleshy stem and broadly oval leaves which are woolly on the under-surface when young. Pure white flowers are produced in small panicles.
P. echinatum is a tuberous species forming a caudex. The succulent stems are erect and few-branched, covered with fleshy spines, while the deciduous leaves are heart-shaped and slightly lobed, dark green above, white-hairy below. The flowers, eight to ten together, are white, pink or purplish lilac, the upper petals sometimes marked with deep carmine or purple. It grows 12–18 in. (30–45 cm) tall.
P. ensatum (P. oblongatum) has a small caudex set above soil level. The hairy leaves on long hairy stems appear before the umbel of flowers, which are pale yellow, striped with red. It is a choice and desirable species.
*P. tetragonum** is a popular plant with a succulent stem and branches, up to 28 in. (70 cm) tall. The stems are three to four-sided, bright green and smooth, and the leaves are broadly heart-shaped and toothed. The flower head usually carries three flowers together, rose-pink with purplish veining on long stems.
Sarcocaulon l'heritieri from Namibia is an erect branching species, with green, waxy white stems bearing small thorns and small heart-shaped leaves. The flowers are pale to bright yellow.
S. multifidum, a spreading bushy species also from Namibia, has almost horizontal branches about 4 in. (10 cm) long and no thorns. Greenish woolly leaves appear in small clusters from the tubercles on the branches. The flowers are bright pink, reddish towards the centre.

LILIACEAE (ALOEACEAE)

The lily family contains many well-known plants, such as lilies, tulips and hyacinths, as well as a large number of decidedly succulent species. WIth few exceptions, all the succulents are easy to grow. Many flower in late winter to early February, so it is wise to maintain a temperature of 50°F (10°C) to ensure flowering. Use an open porous compost, give good light and water moderately throughout the growing season from April to September. If suitable temperatures have been provided, an occasional watering once the flower spikes appear will not go amiss, but choose the brightest days. Propagation is by offsets or seed.

*Aloe arborescens** is from South Africa and Malawi, the African continent being the home of most aloes. This popular species has a rosette of long, fleshy, greenish leaves, 18–24 in. (45–60 cm) tall, with small teeth on the margins. It offsets freely,

quickly forming large clusters. The flowers are reddish, borne on a stout stem in early spring. There is also an attractive variegated form with yellow-striped leaves.
A. aristata* is perhaps the commonest species of the genus. The small rosettes consist of many dark green leaves, which are almost totally covered with regular, minute, soft spines and have whitish edges with tiny horny teeth. Plants offset very freely, rapidly developing into large clumps. The flower spike is up to 20 in. (50 cm) long, bearing clusters of orange-red blooms in late spring and early summer.
A. distans has a creeping stem, often very extended, with a few leaves scattered along the length, but densely arranged at the tip to make an attractive firm rosette. The broadly oval leaves are fresh or bluish green, very succulent, each some 4 in. (10 cm) long and pointed at the tips; they have yellowish horny edges with teeth, which are also evident on the undersurface. The flowering stem is about 16 in. (40 cm) tall with reddish flowers, produced in early spring or sometimes before.
A. variegata,* the popular partridge-breasted aloe, is now apparently almost unknown in the wild. The erect lance-shaped leaves are deep green with white irregular markings and horny whitish margins. Pinkish reddish flowers are carried on a spike about 12 in. (30 cm) high from late spring to early summer.
A. zanzibarica (A. concinna) from the island of Zanzibar is a most attractive species with variegated leaves and a semi-creeping habit. It grows up to 1 ft (30 cm) tall, the leaves forming an elongated rosette. The flower stem is about 8 in. (20 cm) long and bears pale scarlet flowers with greenish edges in summer. It is a very desirable plant and easily grown but, unfortunately, like many dwarf aloes, it is uncommon.
A. zebrina has lance-shaped, fleshy, dark green leaves 6–12 in. (15–30 cm) long, covered with numerous whitish green spots which often merge into transverse bands, the margins with pale brownish teeth. The flower head may be 3¼ ft (1 m) or more tall, carrying a spike of deep red blooms in late summer.
Bulbine frutescens from Cape Province, South Africa, is a fibrous-rooted species with soft, rather fleshy leaves about 8 in. (20 cm) long in a very loose rosette. The raceme of many bright yellow flowers, or sometimes brownish orange or white, appears in late spring. It is of easy culture and offsets freely to form large clumps.
Bulbinopsis semibarbata comes from Australia. It has a fibrous rootstock and thin fleshy leaves in a lax rosette about 6 in. (15 cm) high. Several yellow flowers are held above the leaves in early spring.
Gasteria liliputana* from Cape Province, South Africa, has a spirally arranged rosette of dark green, glossy leaves with pointed tips, 2½ in. (6 cm) long, which are banded with greenish white spots. The pinkish red flowers are on a long stalk in summer.
G. verrucosa* is a variable South African species. The tapering leaves up to 6 in. (15 cm) long are greyish green with numerous white tubercles, giving a roughened surface, and arranged in a semi-rosette. Reddish flowers are borne on a long arching stem in early summer. Plants offset freely to form extensive mats (see p. 112).
Haworthia greenii comes from South Africa, the main habitat of the genus. It is a semi-prostrate plant which offsets from the base to make clumps. The small thick leaves are densely crowded on a stem some 6 in. (15 cm) long and covered in tubercles. The flowers are whitish, in summer.
H. reinwardtii,* with over 20 varieties, is similar to H. greenii. The greenish or brownish green leaves are densely arranged along the stem and mostly covered with many white protuberances.
H. retusa, another variable species, has a rosette made up of small, thick, fleshy leaves, triangular and slightly recurved, which are translucent with whitish green lines. It offsets freely from the base to form clumps.
Xanthorrhoea semiplana is a representative of a small Australian genus. It has a rosette of slender leaves well over 3¼ ft (1 m) long and a compact spike of white flowers on a stem which may be 6½ ft (2 m) high. Plants can be grown from seed and, in cultivation, should remain 'containable' for many years (see p. 79).

Left: Like most aloes, A. *distans* is grown mainly for the handsome foliage
Right: *Aloe variegata* is unusual in having leaves arranged in ranks, not in a rosette

MESEMBRYANTHEMACEAE

This is a huge family containing over 100 genera and numerous species. Some are shrubby, others widespreading, and they include the so-called mimicry plants, such as *Lithops*, which model themselves on their surroundings. The majority are of fairly easy culture, but require care in judging when to water and when to allow them to dry out completely, since they differ in their needs. This aspect of growing 'mesems' is critical: if water is given during the dormant season, plants tend to rot; equally, if they are left too dry during the growing and flowering seasons, they are liable to shrivel. (Individual requirements are indicated in the descriptions below.) Always give them the best possible light and grow in a very porous, but enriched compost with a minimum temperature of 50°F (10°C). The family is based in southern Africa, with a large number of species found in Cape Province. Propagation is easy from seeds or cuttings.

Aloinopsis schooneesii has a tuberous rootstock and small, thick, bluish green leaves grouped in a rough rosette. The flowers are bright yellow striped with red, in late summer and early autumn (see p. 112).
A. setifera forms a tiny rosette about 1¼ in. (3 cm) across. The leaves are triangular, short, thick and wide, the tips edged with minute teeth and tubercles. The flowers are bright yellow, sometimes pinkish. Both *Aloinopsis* species should be kept dry from November to late February.

111

Left: *Gasteria verrucosa* comes from South Africa, as do all members of the genus
Right: *Aloinopsis schooneesii* is dormant in winter, when no water should be given

---

*Carpobrotus acinaciformis** inhabits shady areas near Cape Town, South Africa. The stems are angled and branched with long, succulent, greyish green leaves. The flowers are about 4 in. (10 cm) across in rich carmine-purple, produced in late spring and early summer.

C. edulis is similar, but with longer stems and branches. The leaves are three-angled, up to 5½ in. (12 cm) long, fleshy and bright green. The flowers vary from pale yellow to reddish purple, in summer. Keep the plant fairly dry in winter and water when flower buds appear.

Cephalophyllum alstonii is a prostrate species with long greyish branches. The leaves, in tufts, are cylindrical with the upper surface flattened, greyish green and densely covered with minute, dark green, translucent dots. The flowers are a rich ruby red with distinctive violet stamens, in midsummer. Water from early March to October, but always in moderation.

Chasmatophyllum musculinum is a cushion-forming plant. The greyish or bluish green leaves are three-angled, the upper surface convex and the edges sometimes with minute teeth. The flowers are yellow, in late summer. Keep it dry from November to early March, then water carefully.

Cheiridopsis candidissima is a spreading plant, with leaves developing in pairs, greyish green, somewhat boat-shaped and generally covered with small, dark green dots. The flowers are yellow, in summer.

C. pillansii has small paired leaves, rounded on the outer surface, flat on the inner, which are silvery grey with minute dots of a deeper shade. Golden yellow flowers, about 2½ in. (6 cm) across, are borne on short fleshy stems in summer. Both species require watering from mid-February until November.

Conicosia capensis is a short-lived plant. The stems carry tufted heads of three-angled, green to bluish green leaves, 15 in. (40 cm) long. The flowers, about 2¾ in. (7 cm) across, are pale to canary-yellow.

C. pugioniformis is similar, having more erect stems and leaves greyish with reddish bases. The flowers, usually one to three together from the tops of the branches, are

112

bright sulphur-yellow, in summer. Water these *Conicosia* species freely from April to late October.

Conophytum luisae has tiny heart-shaped bodies (consisting of two thick, united leaves), with short, rounded, greyish green lobes, edged with a darker shade, and the whole is covered with minute darker dots. The flowers are yellow.

C. pearsonii has cone-shaped bodies of glaucous green, with a central cleft which is almost closed and sometimes surrounded with dark dots. It is a beautiful plant, with deep lilac flowers produced in late summer. With all *Conophytum* species, a new body forms within the old body, gradually developing and being sustained by the old body, which eventually dries to leave only a skin. Watering should commence once the new body is apparent and cease by December; it should never be excessive.

Delosperma echinatum is a bushy, much branched plant, with thick, fleshy, bristly leaves. The flowers are white or creamy yellow and can appear at any time throughout the year, but mainly in summer. Water moderately from April to October.

*Dorotheanthus bellidiformis** is the annual 'mesembryanthemum', a very free-flowering plant often used for summer bedding in the garden. The alternate leaves are very fleshy and warty and the flowers appear in a variety of colours – white, pink, red, orange or multicoloured. Water regularly once growth is apparent. (It has now been reclassified in the genus *Cleretum*; see p. 115).

*Faucaria tuberculosa** is typical of many similar plants from Cape Province. The deep green leaves are very thick, about ¾ in. (2 cm) long and the same in width, roughly triangular and set with small teeth on the upper surface and margins. The flowers are pale yellow, about 1½ in. (4 cm) across, in late summer. Water with care from April to October.

Glottiphyllum linguiforme is a well-known species with thick, fleshy, bright green leaves and golden yellow flowers, about 2½ in. (6 cm) across, on short stalks.

G. oligocarpum has short stems bearing four leaves in two rows, thick, fleshy, greyish green and velvety. The flowers are yellow, in summer. Water both species carefully from late March to September.

Kensitia pillansii is one of the less common species from Cape Province. It is a many-branched shrub up to 2 ft (60 cm) tall, with reddish branches clad in three-angled, very succulent, slightly incurved leaves. The flowers are borne singly at the tips of the branches, about 2 in. (5 cm) across, with numerous widespreading petals of reddish purple and white. They appear in summer. It requires much the same treatment as *Lampranthus*.

Lampranthus albus is a semi-shrub about 8 in. (20 cm) high, with fleshy, bluish or bluish white leaves and pure white flowers.

L. aureus has longer, greenish grey leaves and brilliant orange flowers.

L. haworthii has long, fleshy, cylindrical leaves, which are densely grey-woolly. Lilac-purple flowers, up to 2½ in. (7 cm) across, are produced in profusion (see p. 115).

L. purpureus is a much-branched species with glaucous green leaves and purplish flowers.

*L. roseus,** a popular species, has three-angled leaves covered with translucent dots and charming pale pink flowers about 1½ in. (4 cm) in diameter.

L. zeyheri has many curved slender branches with cylindrical leaves of bright green, which are enhanced by bright purple-violet flowers about 2½ in. (6 cm) across, borne singly at the tips of the branches. The *Lampranthus* species have some of the most colourful flowers in the family, produced in summer. All require a rest period from late October until March.

Lapidaria margaretae is less often encountered than other 'mesems'. The tiny leaves are united at the base, usually six to eight together on an extremely short, almost unnoticeable stem, and have a smooth whitish or pinkish surface with reddish

Left: *Lithops pseudotruncatella* var. *volkii*, a widely grown stone or pebble plant
Right: *Ophthalmophyllum latum*, a windowed plant which should be kept dry
from December to late April

margins. The flowers are bright golden yellow, about 2 in. (5 cm) across, in summer.
It requires very careful watering and should be kept dry from late October till April.
Lithops julii has stone-like bodies of whitish grey, about ¾ in. (2 cm) across and
gradually forming clumps. The top surface is grooved with brownish lines and dots
and the flowers are pure white, about 1¼ in. (3 cm) wide. It belongs to one of the
foremost genera in the family – commonly termed stone plants or living stones on
account of their shape and normally having white or yellow flowers. The flowering
period is from July to November and the flowers generally open in the afternoon.
Give the plants good light and a porous compost and keep dry from December to late
April.
L. karasmontana, another interesting and popular white-flowering species, has
cone-shaped bodies which are very wrinkled on top.
*L. leslei** tends to become multi-headed quite quickly. The small bodies are brownish
or reddish green, pitted with brownish and greenish markings and spots on the flat
upper surface. The flowers are bright yellow.
*L. pseudotruncatella** and its varieties are very popular. They have conical,
brownish grey bodies, covered with a network of marbling, veining and dots, which
quickly form groups. The species has golden yellow flowers, while the variety
mundtii has yellowish orange flowers about 1½ in. (4 cm) across, with red tips to the
petals. In the variety *volkii* the bodies are usually arranged in groups of four, each
about 1¼ in. (3 cm) wide, greyish blue with numerous dots of a deeper shade, and the
flowers are yellow.
Nananthus aloides is a low-growing species with tapering, dark green leaves
covered with numerous tubercles and having roughened edges, six to ten together
in a basal tuft. The flowers are yellow, often with a deeper stripe on the petals, and
about 1 in. (2.5 cm) across.
N. transvaalensis is similar, but with shorter leaves, and its dullish green back-
ground colour is emphasized by the prominent bumps along the margins. The
flowers are borne in summer and are bright yellow, each petal having a thin red line
down the centre. Keep these two species completely dry from late October till April.

Left: *Dorotheanthus bellidiformis* is a popular bedding plant, easily raised from seed sown in spring
Right: *Lampranthus haworthii* covers itself in flowers in summer

---

Ophthalmophyllum dinteri has cylindrical bodies up to 1¼ in. (4 cm) high and about ¾ in. (2 cm) wide, with a deep cleft across the top, generally reddish green and the lobes having reddish transparent 'windows'. The flowers are reddish purple and about 1¼ in. (3 cm) wide.

O. latum is similar, the bodies being a pale yellowish green, with slightly warty lobes and deeper greenish dots around the area of the 'windows'. The flowers are pure white. These require the same attention as *Lithops*, to which they are closely related, and they flower in late summer and autumn.

*Pleiospilos bolusii** has thick fleshy bodies consisting of one pair of leaves about 2¾ in. (7 cm) long, greyish green with numerous darker green dots covering the surface. The golden yellow flowers, 2½ in. (6 cm) or more across and often three or four together on short stems, are borne in late summer. Water freely when the plants are in full growth and then keep them dry.

Ruschia modesta grows about 18 in. (45 cm) tall, with long branches each bearing two boat-shaped leaves. The whole is finely covered with protuberances and the very small, deep purple flowers are borne on a short head in summer.

R. namaquana is some 6 in. (15 cm) high with several stiffish branches fairly densely covered with small, greenish, hairy, dotted leaves and many small white flowers.

R. utilis is one of the tallest members of this genus of shrubby plants, often attaining 6½ ft (2 m). It is bushy, with greyish stems and branches, which are densely leafy, and the flowerhead consists of numerous small white flowers. Keep it and its relatives dry from October to March.

Trichodiadema bulbosum has a pronounced tuberous rootstock which, if exposed, resembles the base of a bonsai tree. The stems reach about 8 in. (20 cm) high and the leaves are small, thick and fleshy, greyish green and minutely bristly. The deep crimson flowers are about ¾ in. (2 cm) across, in late autumn.

T. mirabile has stems covered with small bristle-like hairs and cylindrical leaves of bright green with small brownish bristles. The flowers are pure white. All species need only a short period of dormancy from late November to February and flower in late summer and early autumn.

MORACEAE

This interesting family, which includes the fig and mulberry, has just two truly succulent genera and these only in part. However, there are a few unusual succulent species, which are much in demand from connoisseurs. Plants require a rich porous compost, a minimum temperature of 59°F (15°C) and very careful watering, particularly for *Dorstenia*. The flowering time is summer. They can be grown quite successfully from seed or, in some instances, cuttings.

Dorstenia crispa from east Africa has fleshy, slightly swollen, semi-erect stems with a few short branches towards the tips. The leaves are hairy, narrowly tapering, with crisped edges, and some 2¾ in. (7 cm) long. The petalless flower is set on a star-shaped base about ¾ in. (2 cm) across with thickened edges and longer bracts.
D. hildebrandtii developes a small caudex with thickish stems and branches and broadly spear-shaped leaves. The flowers appear from the leaf axils and have a purplish base with deeper purple bracts.
Ficus decaisnei from the Philippines is one of several Far Eastern epiphytic species which can be considered succulent (although the genus is better known for the fig, *F. carica*, and rubber plant, *F. elastica*). It has elliptical fleshy leaves and elongated aerial roots which eventually reach ground level to form bush-like plants.
F. palmeri from Mexico is a tree-like species, although seldom exceeding 3¼ ft (1 m) in cultivation, with a thick caudex-type base and oval downy leaves about 2¾ in. (7 cm) long and 2 in. (5 cm) across. Insignificant whitish flowers are followed by fig-like fruits. When young, it makes an excellent houseplant.

PASSIFLORACEAE

Only one genus in this family, which includes the popular passion flower, contains known succulents. They differ from other members of the family in having a caudex-like base, resembling that of a bonsai tree. A fairly rich, porous compost is advised and water can be applied freely while plants are in growth, but must be withheld during the dormant season. They flower in summer. Give good light and an airy position with a minimum temperature of 50°F (10°C). They are easily grown from seed or cuttings.

Adenia globosa from Kenya has a large stone-like caudex developing several thick erect branches, which are greyish green and spiny. Leaves appear infrequently and, when they do, soon fall. The scented flowers are star-like and bright red.
A. pechuelii from Namibia has a large, fleshy, greenish grey caudex, somewhat bottle-shaped, and many branches with spines. The pale pink flowers are produced in clusters of three at the top.

PEDALIACEAE

A number of genera in this family include succulent species, but only the southern African *Pterodiscus* has achieved any degree of popularity. They are mainly low-growing and given attention, can become very interesting, attractive, flowering plants. A temperature of 55°F (13°C) is advisable, a bright location and careful watering, keeping them completely dry during dormancy. They flower in summer. A rich porous compost, totally lime-free, is necessary. They are easily grown from seed.

Pterodiscus luridus has a rounded caudex, 2 in. (5 cm) or more thick, very fleshy and tapering to a branched point. The plant rarely exceeds 18 in. (45 cm). The numerous leaves along the branches are dark green above, bluish white and woolly below. The flowers are yellow dotted with red.
P. speciosus is seldom more than 6 in. (15 cm) tall. The narrow leaves have toothed edges and the slender funnel-shaped flowers are pale purplish red (see p. 118)

PORTULACACEAE

This is a family of beautiful, colourful plants, many of them popular in the garden, and others are used for greenhouse and home decoration. They include annuals and perennials and the majority can be easily increased from seeds or cuttings. A sunny position is essential for best results and the compost or soil should be rich, open and free from lime. The perennial species require a fairly dry dormant period, but a little water can be given occasionally if the temperature is maintained above 55°F (13°C). They flower in summer.

Anacampseros alstonii is one of the most fascinating species. The base is a flat thick caudex 2¼ in. (6 cm) or so in diameter, from the top of which numerous short fleshy stems emerge, bearing rows of small leaves almost totally concealed in a sheath of silvery white. The flowers protrude well beyond the stems and are pure white. It is an exceedingly choice miniature.
A. australiana from Australia is one of the very few species found outside the African continent. It has a long, thick, tuberous rootstock, with much of the stem underground. The small lance-shaped leaves in a basal rosette are hairy, whitish and very succulent and the flowers are bright pink.
*A. rufescens** from the Karroo, South Africa, has a thick, tuberous, caudex-like rootstock with many erect and spreading stems and branches about 2½ in. (6 cm) long. The thick, spirally arranged leaves are green on the upper surface, reddish below, with yellowish white, bristly hairs almost as long as the leaves. The flowers are deep pink.
Calandrinia grandiflora from Chile grows nearly 3¼ ft (1 m) tall when in full bloom. The oval leaves with pointed tips are green and fleshy, up to 6 in. (15 cm) long and mostly at the base of the plant. The small flowers are bright pale purple, borne in terminal clusters.

Left: The dwarf *Pterodiscus speciosus* requires full exposure to sun
Right: The popular *Lewisia cotyledon* hybrids are available in a wide range of colours

---

C. polyandra occurs in many parts of Australia. Up to 20 in. (50 cm) tall, it has several erect stems with succulent, greyish green leaves and racemes of deep pink flowers.
Lewisia cotyledon is from northern California. The species and its many hybrids are well known in cultivation, usually being treated as alpines. The leaves are arranged in a basal rosette about 4 in. (12 cm) in diameter and may be quite fleshy or softer, with or without toothed margins. The flowers in panicles on stems 4 in. (10 cm) long are white or pink and veined in shades of red. The Sunset strain is one of the best. Lewisias do well if planted on their sides in a wall and are easily propagated from the plentiful seed.
L. rediviva is similar, with a long, tapering, fleshy rootstock which is said to be edible, narrow fleshy leaves and large white flowers.
*Portulaca grandiflora** – or, rather, its hybrids – is commonly grown in gardens as a half-hardy annual and is available in a vast array of colours with both single and double flowers. The true species is found in the Windward Islands of the Caribbean; it is widespreading with slender leaves and has red single or double flowers on 6 in. (15 cm) stems. The sun plants, as they are sometimes called, thrive in rather poor, dry soil (see also p. 72).
*Portulacaria afra** from South Africa is a shrubby plant with many branches. The leaves are small, glossy green and almost circular and, like the stems and branches, are obviously succulent. The very small, inconspicuous flowers are pinkish. There is also an attractive variegated form.

VITACEAE

The succulent species of this family originate mainly from Africa, including Madagascar, and many have a caudiciform base, which has helped to account for their popularity. The flowers, borne in summer, are less interesting than the fruits. These resemble grapes (grapevine is a member of the family), but are usually smaller in

Left: The annual *Portulaca grandiflora* opens its flowers only in a sunny position
Right: The variegated form of *Portulacaria afra* makes an attractive foliage houseplant

---

size and in the number of fruits to a cluster. A really porous compost is essential and preferably one rich in humus. Plants need a bright, not necessarily sunny position and should be freely watered during the growing season, but kept completely dry during dormancy. A minimum temperature of 50°F (10°C) is required.

*Cissus quadrangularis** from east Africa is well known and has climbing four-angled stems with wing-like edges. The stems are divided into segments and the leaves appear at the nodes, being thick, three-lobed and with toothed margins. The fruits are black.

Cyphostemma seitziana has grape-like fruits

C. rotundifolia is from the Transvaal and also known in Saudi Arabia. It has more rounded leaves with smooth edges and the fruits are green, becoming red.
Cyphostemma bainesii from Namibia has a bottle-shaped caudex about 10 in. (25 cm) thick and 2 ft (60 cm) tall and a few stout branches towards the top, the whole enveloped in a greenish skin. The leaves are about 4½ in. (12 cm) long and covered with minute hairs.
C. seitziana is a taller species and has long, oval, fleshy, greyish green leaves with serrated margins. The fruits are yellowish becoming reddish (see p. 119).

Mother-in-law's tongue, *Sansevieria trifasciata* var. *laurentii*, has long been grown as a houseplant

Pests and Diseases

Most pests and diseases can be conveniently dealt with by applying suitable pesticides and fungicides, which are available under various trade names. However, the fact must never be overlooked that pesticides and fungicides are potentially toxic. Always handle them with extreme care, use only as instructed on the container and, above all, keep them out of reach of children and pets. Some succulents may be damaged by pesticides. Avoid treating plants while they are exposed to bright sunlight or high temperatures or are very dry at the roots.

PESTS

Inspect your plants carefully at regular intervals so that any pests are detected before a heavy infestation has developed. If they are already infested, treat the plants as indicated below; the treatment should be repeated at intervals of five to seven days until all signs of the pests are gone, followed by a thorough overhead spray with slightly tepid water, to wash away dead insects which might still remain on stems or leaves.

The pests most likely to be encountered are comparatively few, but all can prove a danger unless destroyed.

Mealybug
These small insects are covered with a whitish waxy substance. They lay their eggs in rather concealed places, always in clusters, and these too have a white waxy-woolly coating. One method of dealing speedily with them is to take a fine paint brush, dip it in insecticidal soap and remove the waxy coating on the insects and eggs, without which they will not survive. Then, after a thorough cleansing with tepid water sprayed overhead, treat with malathion to help avoid further infestations. Some plants, e.g. *Crassula*, may be damaged by pesticides. An alternative treatment during the summer is to introduce a ladybird beetle, *Cryptolaemus montrouzieri*, which is available by mail order from various suppliers.

Root mealybug
This pest is less easy to detect and the tendency is for plants to be

attacked during the dormant season. If they suggest poor growth or become weary-looking or fail to flower, there is every reason to suspect something is wrong at the roots. Carefully remove the plant from its pot and you may discern a whitish 'mould' adhering to both the soil and the inner surface of the pot. This is wax secreted by root mealybug. The whole lot can be washed away with tepid water containing malathion and the plant should be repotted in fresh compost. Towards the end of the growing season, give a application of malathion, standing the pot in the solution until the compost is really saturated, and then allow the soil to dry out for the period of dormancy.

Scale insects

These tiny sap-feeding pests have a limpet-like shell covering of brownish or greyish brown. When they reach the adult stage, they cease to move. Eggs are laid and hatched under the shell or scale and the resulting larvae seek suitable feeding sites and themselves become immobile. They can be carefully scraped away or, when the scales are newly hatched, may be removed with a soft cloth or brush dipped in insecticidal soap. Alternatively, the use of a spray containing malathion will be very satisfactory.

Whitefly and aphids

These are persistent and dangerous pests for certain succulents. Several sprays are available, such as insecticidal soaps, permethrin or bifenthrin, that can be used for indoor plants. Whitefly can also be controlled by introducing the parasitic chalcid wasp, Encarsia formosa and this is often the best control during the summer months due to the widespread occurrence of pesticide-resistant strains of whitefly. Pirimicarb can be used to control aphids without harming the whitefly parasite.

Red spider mite

These minute reddish, yellowish or black pests colonize and surround themselves with very fine webs. They feed from the stems and leaves by piercing the epidermis and sucking the sap, frequently causing a mottled, discolouration of the plant generally. Since they appear to flourish in a dry atmosphere, reasonable humidity plus good ventilation can discourage this pest. Sprays containing bifenthrin, malathion or pirimiphos-methyl can be used to deal with attacks. Biological control with the predatory mite, Phytoseiulus persimilis, is an effective alternative. (Addresses of suppliers of biological controls are available from the Entomologist at the RHS Garden, Wisley, tel. 01483 224234.)

Sciarid fly

Also known as mushroom fly or fungus gnat, this pest has become more prevalent with the popularity of peat-based composts. The minute greyish brown flies lay their eggs in the compost, which hatch out into thin whitish grubs with black heads that feed on the roots of seedlings and mature plants alike. Insecticides containing malathion or permethrin are recommended as sprays bore into the base of cuttings. Yellow sticky traps hung above the plants will capture many adult flies.

Vine weevil

The grubs are plump white maggots with light brown heads, up to $\frac{1}{2}$ in. (1 cm) long. They live in the soil, where they destroy roots and bore into the base of succulents, especially in the autumn to spring period. The adults are slow-moving dull black beetles, which are active at night during the spring and summer. The older grubs are difficult to control as they are tolerant of most pesticides. Plants can be given protection by drenching the compost with pathogenic nematodes (*Heterorhabditis* or *Steinernema* sp.) in August and September. Look for and destroy adult weevils hiding under pots, leaves and greenhouse staging, particularly during the spring and early summer. Infested plants should be repotted in fresh compost, although the root damage may be so severe that it is better to propagate new plants from cuttings.

DISEASES

Diseases with succulents are mainly confined to black rot and damping off, the latter being largely a problem with seedlings.

Black rot

This is likely to be in evidence with many of the Asclepiadaceae, such as *Stapelia* and kindred genera. A blackening of the stem becomes apparent at more or less soil level, which is caused by bacteria penetrating the stems and turning the tissues black and soft. If noted at an early stage, the affected parts can be cut away with a sharp knife.

Damping off

This can be prevented by the use of a copper-based fungicide such as Cheshunt Compound. Mix it with water and lightly spray seedlings at the first watering following germination.

Above: *Orbea* (*Stapelia*) *variegata* is one of the most widely grown members of the Asclepiadaceae
Below: *Hoya carnosa* 'Tricolor' needs a semi-shaded position

Above: *Kensitia pillansii* from South Africa is the sole species of the genus, and is of shrub-like habit (see p.113)
Below: The thick fleshy leaves of *Glottiphyllum oligocarpum* are typical of all species in the genus (see p.113)

Bromeliads

BILL WALL
revised by CLIVE INNES

Neoregelia macwilliamsii A rare and unusual species found wild within a restricted, shoreline area of Rio de Janeiro, Brazil

Introduction

The bromeliad family comprises well in excess of 2,000 species in more than 50 genera, all originating from South and Central America and the southern states of the USA. The only exception is for a solitary species of *Pitcairnia, P. feliciana,* which was discovered in West Africa in 1937.

They have a common growth habit, the few or many leaves forming a rosette, which may be upright or flat, and in some cases making a cup in the centre that holds water, as in the familiar *Aechmea fasciata* or urn plant. Given such a large number of species, it is not surprising that bromeliads are found in widely different situations: they are distributed in nature at altitudes ranging from sea level in the tropics to the heights of the southern American Andes, living in conditions of high humidity on the forest floor or in arid desert and growing on trees or in the ground.

As a result, bromeliads vary enormously in appearance, from the tiny mat-forming rosettes of *Abromeitiella* to the giant *Brocchinia* and *Puya.* Within the genus *Tillandsia* alone there is great variation, from hard stiff-leaved plants growing on cacti, to the notable lichen-like Spanish moss, *T. usneoides,* which hangs from trees and is so characteristic of the moist southern states of the USA.

The flower heads of bromeliads are also very diverse, with the small white flowers of *Cryptanthus* almost hidden in the leaf axils, the flamboyant red and yellow flower spikes of *Guzmania,* the blue and green of *Puya* and the yellow flowers that protrude from waxy-looking bract spikes of *Vriesea.* All, though, are characterized botanically by having three-petalled flowers and three-celled ovaries. The flower spike, with very few exceptions, appears from the centre of the rosette and, after flowering, the rosette ceases to grow but produces new plants from dormant buds found in the leaf axils.

The leaves of the majority of species have tiny shield-like scales, which are able to absorb moisture from the air and help the plant survive drought or extreme heat. Some bromeliads have only two scales at the base of each leaf, while others have numerous scales

Tillandsia usneoides is well-named with its moss-like strands of rootless stems and slender, cylindrical greyish leaves (see p.150)

forming grey bands across the leaves. In many *Tillandsia*, the leaf surface is almost entirely covered with scales, giving the whole plant a silver scurfy appearance.

THE FIRST BROMELIADS

The first bromeliad introduced to Britain was the pineapple, *Ananas comosus*, in 1690. Originally from Brazil, it has become widely cultivated as a cash crop. In Victorian times it was grown to perfection in hothouses and specially constructed hotbeds of manure, to grace the tables of the wealthy.

Further introductions followed slowly and large collections had been established in Europe by the end of the nineteenth century. Sadly, during the two world wars, these were gradually dispersed and lost, although some of the hybrids produced then do still exist today and stocks have also been renewed from those that survived.

Since the 1940s, hundreds of new species have been introduced into cultivation, both in Europe and the USA. As bromeliads are readily hybridized and grown from seed, numerous hybrids have been raised too, not only within a particular genus but between different genera, such as *Aechmea* × *Neoregelia* and *Cryptanthus* × *Billbergia*. Bromeliads have become increasingly popular and are now common as houseplants and for decorating foyers, offices and shopping complexes. They are tough plants, able to withstand some neglect and still remain colourful. The number of plants available commercially has greatly increased and, whereas in 1950 it would have been quite difficult to obtain examples of more than a dozen species, today one could collect 300 or more different bromeliad species and their hybrids.

GLOSSARY

axil: angle formed by junction of leaf and stem
bract: modified leaf between the flower and the leaves
epiphytic: tree-dwelling, but not parasitic
peltate: shield-like, not attached at the edges
saxicolous: growing on rocks
stolon: strong sucker-like stem
terrestrial: growing on the ground
xerophytic: existing with little water

Tillandsia ionantha is a readily available, small, compact plant. The brilliantly coloured flowers last for several weeks (see p.148)

General Cultivation

IN A GREENHOUSE OR CONSERVATORY

Temperature

Bromeliads may be grown to perfection in a greenhouse or conservatory. The range of plants that can be accommodated depends on the winter minimum temperature. If this is maintained at 60°F (15°C), then all the species and hybrids will succeed. A lower temperature of 50°F (10°C) will limit the number to some extent and 40°F (5°C) even more, although there is still a wide choice of plants. The temperature requirements of individual plants are given in their descriptions in each chapter. As a rough guide, the softer-leaved kinds need a higher temperature, while those with very hard, stiff leaves are much more tolerant of cold. The soft-leaved types include Guzmania, most Vriesea and some of the Aechmea and Tillandsia. Cryptanthus are also warmth-loving, originating as they do from the forest floor. In a cool greenhouse, most Aechmea, Billbergia, Neoregelia, Dyckia and Puya can be grown and many of the grey-leaved xerophytic (existing with little water) Tillandsia. The intermediate temperature allows numerous Aechmea, Nidularium and Pitcairnia to be added to those listed for the cool greenhouse.

Light

Under glass, we can provide the right environment for any bromeliad by careful positioning. Some light shading, as produced by a coat of Summercloud on the outside of the glass, is advisable to prevent direct sunshine scorching the plants. Place the light-loving xerophytic Tillandsia and Dyckia and the hard-leaved Aechmea and Billbergia high up, where they get most light, followed in decreasing order of light intensity by Neoregelia, Pitcairnia, Guzmania, soft-leaved Aechmea and Tillandsia, Nidularium and Cryptanthus. All bromeliads will grow in shade or semi-shade, but the stiff-leaved types have a much better shape and leaf colour when given plenty of light; on the other hand, many of the coloured-leaved

The soft-leaved Vriesea nana does best in good light

133

Vriesea and *Guzmania* bleach and lose their exotic appearance in too much light. Light, therefore, is one of the most important factors in bromeliad culture.

Composts, potting and watering

Moisture is also important. The xerophytic *Tillandsia* or air plants are characterized by grey-scaled leaves and are epiphytic (tree-dwelling) in nature, most of them relying on heavy dews at night for water. Under glass, it is necessary to ensure extremely rapid drainage of excess water and good air circulation, thus enabling them to dry out and allowing the peltate (shield-like) scales on the leaves to retain sufficient moisture for the plants to use for a day or so. They are best grown mounted on a piece of bark or branch hung up in the greenhouse (see p.136).

Other bromeliads, like *Dyckia* and *Hechtia*, are succulent terrestrial (growing on the ground) plants and can store water in their fleshy leaves for some time. They should be potted into a very open compost of equal volumes of coarse sand and moss peat and watered only when completely dry.

The remaining bromeliads – the majority – can be grown in pots using a mixture of coarse sand and moss peat in equal volumes, plus half a part of leafmould. This affords the free drainage they all need. The compost should always be allowed to dry out between waterings and feeding with a high potash liquid fertilizer, such as are recommended for tomatoes, at every third watering will bring out the best colour in the leaves, without producing a lot of soft leaf growth. Plastic or clay pots may be used. Clay is particularly suitable for bromeliads, since it permits air to reach the roots – an important factor with epiphytic plants, which most bromeliads are. In addition, clay is heavier than plastic and makes the plants much more stable in their pots.

In the greenhouse or conservatory, particularly with a large permanent collection, the easiest method of watering is a hose-pipe fitted with a spray nozzle. The central cup or vase of bromeliads can be flushed out with plenty of water, to prevent possible stagnation when the flower spike has finished flowering and is beginning to rot away. The question is often asked whether the cup of a bromeliad should be kept full of water. There is in fact no need to do so, but water must be supplied to the roots as with all other plants. Water that does get into the cup will not hurt the plant and under normal conditions helps to maintain some humidity. However, if the temperature is likely to fall below 40°F (5°C) at any time, the liquid should be tipped out, otherwise a 'cold burn' may

Nidularium species, such as *N. fulgens*, require temperatures above 50°F (10°C) (see p.171)

form on the foliage at the level of the water, which will show as a brown line across each leaf when the plant has grown on.

Permanent planting

An excellent way to grow bromeliads in the greenhouse or conservatory is in a permanent bed specially designed for them. This is easily constructed with wooden boards about 9 in. (23 cm) wide, which are placed on the floor of the greenhouse to make a rectangular frame of the required size. Set a couple of dead tree branches or artificial trees (see below) in the middle and then put a layer of broken brick in the bottom of the frame to a depth of about 3 in. (7.5 cm). Finally, fill the frame with a mixture of equal volumes of coarse sand and moss peat. The trees may be planted with *Tillandsia* and other epiphytic plants and the bed below can house the more shade-loving bromeliads. Many other plants, like begonias, gesnerias and ferns, will also thrive in such a planting.

Making a bromeliad tree

As suggested earlier, a small 'tree' is very good for displaying bromeliads in the greenhouse or conservatory or even in the home. It can be simply made with cork bark, which is available from florists and garden centres.

For a small artificial tree $2\frac{1}{2}$ ft (75 cm) or so high, make up a framework of crumpled chicken wire to the rough shape of tree desired. Place the bottom of the framework in a mixture consisting of two parts of sand to one of cement, in a 5 in. (12.5 cm) half-pot, and leave it to dry for a day or two. The plastic half-pot can then be removed, having served its function as a mould. This gives a 'tailor's dummy' on to which sections of cork bark can be wired, using a silicone sealant or adhesive. Make sure the lower pieces of bark are well attached to the cement base. Next, cover any gaps or holes between the pieces of bark by pinning on strips of polythene sheet. The tree may then be filled with a polymeric foam filler, which is sold by DIY shops for thermal insulation. To use it, two chemicals are mixed together and the resultant foaming liquid is poured into the inside of the tree, where it quickly expands and hardens to fill all the spaces and give a rigid structure. After an hour, unpin the pieces of polythene and trim off any excess hardened foam with a knife. Visible foam surfaces can be painted brown to blend with the cork bark. An alternative method is to pack the bark tree with chunks of plastic foam, of the type used for cushions.

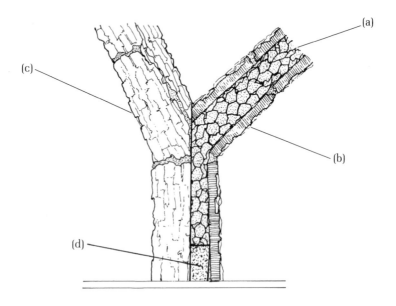

Construction of a bromeliad tree; (a) crumpled wire mesh framework; (b) interior filled with foam plastic; (c) cork bark; (d) cement base

Provision should be made for medium-sized bromeliads by nailing on some curved pieces of bark to form pockets, which will contain the roots. *Aechmea, Billbergia, Neoregelia* and *Nidularium* can be planted in these pockets, using a mixture of sphagnum moss and moss peat and covering the surface with a layer of sphagnum moss alone. Epiphytic and xerophytic plants are prepared by covering their roots with a ball of sphagnum moss and tying or nailing these to the bark tree. Some of the very grey-leaved *Tillandsia* may be attached simply by tying them on to the bark with nylon thread or wire. They should never be glued in position.

Once it is assembled and planted, water the whole tree thoroughly, using a can fitted with a fine rose, and allow it to drain. If intended for the home, the tree is best stood in a saucer or dish to avoid marking the shelf or table underneath it. Further watering should be carried out at intervals, according to the appearance of the sphagnum moss. When the moss is green and obviously damp, water is not needed, but when it becomes whitish in colour and crisp to the touch, water should be given. Rainwater is preferable, using a fine spray and making sure that the whole assembly is soaked. The addition of a high potash liquid fertilizer at every third watering is recommended.

Planted with bromeliads that remain fairly compact, the tree will last for several years and may be moved about between greenhouse and home without difficulty. Good plants for the purpose are the smaller *Billbergia, Cryptanthus, Vriesea carinata, Guzmania lingulata,* × *Cryptbergia rubra,* the dwarf *Neoregelia* and, if the tree can be kept in a very light position, the grey-leaved *Tillandsia.* In a greenhouse, larger plants of many genera may also be accommodated.

IN THE HOME

Bromeliads are ideal houseplants. They are colourful and long-lasting in flower, often with coloured foliage as well. The leaves are resilient and not easily damaged and the plants are tolerant of a wide range of temperature, humidity and light conditions, even putting up with erratic watering, to which houseplants are often subjected. They are generally bought in flower, sometimes with instructions from the florist to water only the central cup and not the compost in the pot. They should, however, be treated just like other plants, watering the compost when necessary – that is, when it has become dry. There is no need to keep the centre of a plant like *Aechmea fasciata* full of water, particularly if there is any risk of it being accidentally knocked over on to the carpet!

Many bromeliads are purchased on sight and then thrown away when the flower spike becomes brown, usually after weeks or even months of display. However, a plant can easily be kept, in order to grow offsets and produce new plants (see p.141). Alternatively, it may be grown into a bigger multi-headed plant. To do this, remove the old flower and repot the plant in a pot 2 in. (5 cm) larger than the previous one. As the flower spike begins to die off, offsets will be produced from the leaf axils. Continue watering as normal and give a high potash fertilizer at every third watering. The old flower spike should be removed once it is dead and, whenever any of the old leaves begin to die back, these too may be detached, although many of them will persist and remain in good condition for some months. After about a year in the case of *Aechmea fasciata*, the plant will have formed a two- or three-headed specimen which, if kept in a fairly light position, may well produce a flower spike from each of the rosettes in their second year. Other commonly offered species and hybrids of *Aechmea, Guzmania, Neoregelia, Nidularium* and *Vriesea* may be treated in the same way, apart from *Vriesea splendens*, the flaming sword, which is usually grown from seed to flower and then discarded.

Almost without exception, bromeliads are very easy house-plants. The various species and hybrids of *Billbergia* are probably the toughest of all and will stand the lowest temperatures, while *Vriesea, Guzmania* and *Cryptanthus* revel in warm conditions. In recent years, a large number of xerophytic *Tillandsia* have become available, mounted on various bases like seashells and pieces of driftwood (although I am rather apprehensive about the use of shells because of their alkaline reaction). These air plants should thrive and flower if they are kept in a light position indoors and dipped or sprayed with rainwater daily, adding liquid fertilizer to the water at every third watering during the summer.

Further information about cultivation, together with brief descriptions of some readily available plants, is given in the chapters devoted to specific groups and genera.

Above: *Neoregelia meyendorffii* var. *tricolor* may be kept and grown on into a larger plant (see p.170)
Below: The dwarf *Tillandsia ionantha* var. scaposa is usually grown on a piece of bark

Propagation

Bromeliads are propagated by means of offsets or from seed.

OFFSETS

The easiest, almost foolproof way to increase bromeliads is by off-sets or 'pups', produced from a plant usually just before and for some time after flowering. This is, of course, the only method of propagating particular forms, such as variegated ones, and named hybrids.

With most bromeliads, the flower spike arises from the centre of the tube or rosette that makes up the plant and, having flowered, the rosette will not flower again. After flowering time, the plant begins to grow suckers from one or more of its lower leaf axils. Some species produce their pups close to the axils, while others have a long woody stem or stolon bearing a new rosette at its tip (see illustrations p. 142). Whatever the habit, when a pup has reached about a third of the size of its parent rosette, it may be detached quite easily with a sideways pressure of the thumb. It should then be potted into a mixture of equal volumes of coarse sand and moss peat in a small pot, watered in and grown on in the normal conditions suitable for the plant concerned. Subsequent watering is carried out at intervals and only when the compost is dry. Be careful not to allow water into the centre of the new rosette before it is rooted, or it might become 'blind' and will not grow on. Even so, a blind pup will in time produce its own small offset, which will become your new plant, although later than if it had been the original pup.

Offsets may also be rooted while they are still attached to the parent plant. When the pup has attained about one quarter of the size of the parent, the stolon is covered with a peat and sand mixture for a month or so. Roots form very freely from the bottom of the pup and it is taken off and potted up once it is obviously growing in its own right.

A plant generally produces one to three pups initially and, even after these have been removed, the parent can be retained. Its

Guzmania zahnii has a brilliant flower spike which stays colourful for weeks (see p.179)

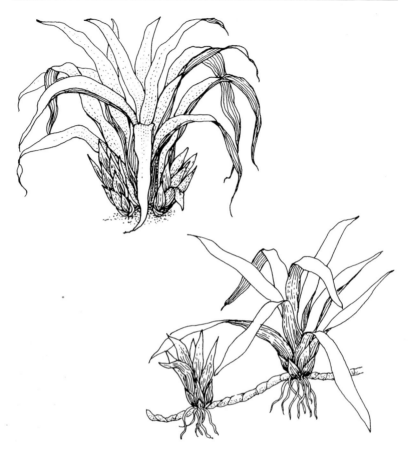

Above: A typical billbergia with offsets produced from near the base of the parent plant
Below: A bromeliad which makes new rosettes at the end of long stolons is characteristic of the creeping types of *Neoregelia*

leaves may become rather tatty, but they can be trimmed back so that the plant takes up a minimum of space. The old stump will last anything up to three or four years, during which time it will produce further pups at intervals, with the possibility of giving one pup from a bud at the base of every leaf. The offsets will root in a peat and sand mixture at any time of year, provided the temperature is suitable for the particular plant being propagated.

The time taken for the new plants to come into flower varies with the species. Most *Billbergia* and a few *Aechmea* will flower one year after detaching the offset, remembering that each type has its own season of flowering. Others take two years, including many of the smaller *Aechmea, Neoregelia, Nidularium, Guzmania* and *Vriesea,* and *Tillandsia* take anything from one to ten years.

Vriesea splendens and one or two closely related species are rather different in their behaviour. After flowering, they form only one offset, from a bud near the centre of the old rosette, which is difficult to remove and root separately. As it grows, the old leaves tend to die off fairly quickly and the new growth is left on the old stump to grow on and flower. For this reason, plants are usually raised from seed.

Cryptanthus species and hybrids produce their offsets liberally from the leaf axils, in some cases without the parent plant coming into flower. The tiny pups are very easily detached – in fact they almost fall off by themselves – and, if potted into a peat and sand mixture, will grow and even produce pups themselves without developing any roots. *Cryptanthus* generally like warm moist conditions and seem to need a bottom heat of about 65°F (18°C) to form a good root system.

The grey-leaved xerophytic, epiphytic *Tillandsia* species may also be increased by offsets, but not as simply as with most other bromeliads. After flowering, minute 'buds' are produced between the more basal leaves or from the stem of the parent plant. These will develop into offsets and if left undisturbed until they attain about half the size of the adult plant, it is likely that they will each have made a couple of wiry roots. At this stage the lower leaves of the parent plant should be carefully removed to expose the pups which can be 'teased' away and tied or stuck to a piece of bark or wood.

SEED

Bromeliad seeds are of three kinds. *Aechmea, Billbergia* and related genera form small berries after the flowers have been fertilized, which are full of a sticky jelly enclosing the seeds. This jelly must be washed off the seeds before they are dried and sown, preferably rinsing them first with a solution of half-strength fungicide to prevent any fungal growths. Other bromeliads, like *Pitcairnia* and the terrestrial *Puya* and *Dyckia*, produce seed capsules containing free dry seeds that are easily harvested. Finally, epiphytic plants such as *Tillandsia, Vriesea* and *Guzmania* have dry seeds with silken parachutes, rather like dandelion seed, which are dispersed by the wind in nature.

Non-winged bromeliad seeds of the first two types can be sown on the surface of a mixture of equal parts of fine moss peat and coarse sand, the compost half filling a small plastic tray, and should be lightly watered with a very fine rose, adding fungicide to the water. Place a sheet of glass over the tray, cover this with a sheet of paper and put it in a heated propagator at 70°–80°F (21–26°C). Germination normally takes from one to three weeks, during which time the seed bed should be kept moist but not soggy, watering with a fungicide solution.

Once the seeds have germinated, the sheet of paper should be removed and, as the seedlings grow, the glass may be gradually opened from the tray, still keeping this in the propagator. When the seedlings reach a height of about 1 in. (2.5 cm), transplant them to a 3 in. (7.5 cm) pot, spacing them about ⅜ in. (1 cm) apart in a compost of moss peat and coarse sand in equal volumes. The pot should be returned to the propagator for a week or so, after which the seedlings can be hardened off to a temperature of about 60°F (15°C). Keep the pot in a lightly shaded position, water only when almost dry and feed with a half-strength liquid fertilizer at every third watering, until the seedlings are large enough to pot on into individual 3 in. (7.5 cm) pots of the same compost.

Winged seeds of the third type are treated differently. They are sown on the surface of a mixture of sharp sand and chopped live sphagnum moss, alternatively, especially with grey-leaved *Tillandsia* species, on a bundle of moistened rough-barked twigs of a conifer such as *Thuja*, and kept fairly shaded and moist in a heated propagator at 70°–80°F (21°–26°C). Humidity is the great essential! This combined with a regular use of a fungicide such as Cheshunt Compound will help provide against damping off. Seedlings may be slow-growing and may take several months to reach sufficient size to be transplanted. Therefore when large enough, they should be taken from their germination site and the xerophytic varieties affixed to pieces of cork bark or gnarled driftwood. Others, such as *Vriesea splendens* or larger, stronger plants of *Tillandsia* – *T. lindenii* is a good example – should be set in a moss-peat and sharp sand mixture. Leave all these seedlings in a propagator for several weeks until thoroughly rooted and established. Then grow them on in a lightly shaded position at 65°F (18°C), feeding with a half-strength liquid fertilizer at every third watering or spraying.

Pests and Diseases

Bromeliads are remarkably free from diseases. As very young seedlings, they may be overcome occasionally by mould, but the use of a suitable fungicide (see p.144) at this early stage is an effective control.

Once plants are about three months old, the danger of fungal attack seems to be past, but it is important that they are grown at the appropriate temperature for the particular plants. Tropical plants like *Vriesea* and *Guzmania* can rot at the crown if subjected to very low temperatures, say 40°F (5°C), particularly if water is retained in the centre. However, it is recognized that temperatures as high as 100°F (37°C) fortunately do not seem to trouble bromeliads at all.

Scale insects
Scale insects will attack bromeliads, appearing as greyish white or yellowish brown, small, round or oval limpet-like objects on the leaves. The young insects are able to move about freely and spread across the leaves and to other plants, before settling down to produce a batch of young. They multiply rapidly and not only make a plant very unsightly, by producing yellow spots on the leaves where they suck the sap, but greatly weaken it if allowed to accumulate, which they can do at the base of the clasping leaves of a bromeliad. Treatment for scale insects consists of spraying with malathion or, better still, spraying with one of the modern systemic insecticides, always following the manufacturer's instructions given on the packaging. If this is done it is possible to eliminate them quite easily.

Mealybugs
Mealybug and more particularly root mealybug, which are both characterized by their cotton-wool protective covering, may be dealt with in the same way.

Slugs and snails
These will eat young seedlings if given the chance. They often find a home in the damp, clasping, leaf bases of the rosettes of adult plants, from which they emerge at night to feast on the flower spikes (not usually the leaves, which happily seem to be too tough) or on other plants. Use slug bait if necessary.

Tillandsia: the Air-Plants

This genus of well in excess of 400 species is the largest of the family. Their habitats range from southern USA and Mexico through to Central and South America to Argentina, also known in many of the West Indian islands. Natural conditions vary tremendously, from cloud and rain forests to dry, somewhat arid, desert-like regions. With but few exceptions they are epiphytic; the exceptions are just a small number of large species found growing on rocks (saxicolous). Keeping in mind their cultural requirements, it is advisable to divide the genus into three main groups which are easily distinguished by their general appearance.

GREY AND SILVERY-LEAVED PLANTS

This group comprises those many species commonly known as air or atmospheric plants. They are undoubtedly among the most adaptable and fascinating of the bromeliads – and, perhaps the most peculiar. Most tillandsias available in Britain are of this xerophytic/epiphytic type – that is, existing with little water. They are mainly small with greyish leaves, the grey colouring being due to a covering of peltate scales which constitute the water-absorbing mechanism of the plants. Watering, therefore, amounts to daily spraying, preferably with rain-water, just sufficient to wet the leaves thoroughly. The addition of a high potash fertilizer at half the recommended rate to the water at every third watering during the warmest months is advisable. A minimum winter temperature of 50°F (10°C) is adequate for the majority of this group, with just a few being able to withstand temperatures down to freezing point if kept dry. They need a light, bright position in the home or greenhouse at all times of the year, but not in direct sun. Good air circulation is advisable and a moist atmosphere, especially at night, is conducive to good growth.

Being both epiphytic and xerophytic, these species may prove difficult to grow in pots, which may prevent the roots and bases from drying out quickly enough, although they can be treated in the same way as orchids using shredded bark or osmunda fibre as the

Tillandsia lindenii is a spectacular plant, but sometimes reluctant to flower (see p.151)

147

potting medium. Better to tie them to pieces of cork bark or branch sections, where they will soon develop a few strong anchoring roots with which to attach themselves firmly. Most of the plants offered for sale were originally imported from the wild, but in these days are freely propagated by specialist nurserymen, mainly from offsets or seed.

Tillandsias are all most acceptable plants for home and greenhouse, and once they are totally mature will produce their attractive spikes and colourful flowers.

T. argentea. A tufted plant, from Central America and the West Indies, this has numerous, narrow, silver-grey leaves 3 in. (7.5 cm) long. The flower spike is 6 in. (15 cm) tall, with about six pale violet florets.

T. brachycaulos. This species has a dense rosette of some 30 leaves, 6 to 9 in. (15–23 cm) long, heavily scaled and silver tinged with red-brown. A dense head of lilac flowers is borne in the centre in spring. It is found over a wide area of Mexico and Central America.

T. bulbosa. This is a tillandsia with a bulb-like base. It has a tubular rosette and the silver-grey leaves flare out at the top. It is very variable, ranging in height from 2 in. to 1 ft (5–30 cm). The flower spike consists of two to eight blue or violet flowers held just above the leaves in summer.

T. caulescens. This Peruvian species develops a branching, woody stem, up to 1½ ft (45 cm) long. At the end is a tuft of 4 in. (10 cm) grey leaves, from which appears a spike of about a dozen white flowers with red bracts.

T. crocata. This has almost round silver-grey leaves about 6 in. (15 cm) long and produces a spike of a few yellow flowers with green bracts in the late summer. It needs care in watering and strong light (see p.151).

T. gardnerii. This is 10 in. (25 cm) in diameter, with curving, narrow, grey-scaled leaves, and produces a compound spike of 4 to 12 heads of rose and lavender flowers in summer.

T. ionantha. This is one of the smallest species and is readily available. A compact plant about 2 in. (5 cm) high and the same across, it has 30 to 40 very stiff, silver-grey, pointed leaves and will make a tight clump in a few years. At flowering time, in late spring, the whole plant becomes brilliant red, while purple and red flowers with prominent anthers protrude from the centre of the rosette. The colour lasts for several weeks. It is robust and will succeed with a winter temperature of 40°F (5°C) (see p.130).

T. plumosa. This is very silvery and feathery in appearance and has a dense head of violet flowers in late summer. A beautiful Mexican species, it makes a rosette only 2 in. (5 cm) in diameter.

T. stricta. Slightly larger, this forms a ball about 3 in. (7.5 cm) in diameter, composed of 50 to 60 narrow, recurving, grey leaves. In May it bears a 3 in. (7.5 cm) spike of pink and purple flowers, persisting for two weeks or so. This is usually followed by two or three offsets from among the basal leaves, which themselves will flower the following year. It is easily grown and will withstand a temperature of 40°F (5°C) (see p.152).

Air plants are effectively displayed on shapely pieces of wood. Here *Tillandsia ionantha* plants have anchored themselves on manzanita wood

Tillandsia brachycaulos is one of the epiphytic species which should be grown on bark, with good air circulation (see p.148)

T. usneoides. One of the most amazing plants of all is a Spanish moss, which forms long festoons of grey-green matted stems and leaves. The individual strands are almost hair-like but, if examined closely, they prove to have typical *Tillandsia* leaves covered with small moisture-retaining scales and produce miniature, three-petalled, greenish white flowers. The bundles of stems are easily divided to make new festoons. In cultivation, it will stand low temperatures, down to 40°F (5°C), but it is essential to provide plenty of fresh air. Water both morning and evening, with rainwater if possible, and grow it in a light position, draped over a branch or similar support (see p.128).

PARTLY SCALE-LEAVED PLANTS

There are a few species of *Tillandsia* with thin, somewhat scaled leaves that are often available as houseplants in pots. They can be grown to flowering size in 4 in. (10 cm) pots of a peat and sand mixture and should be watered when dry, fertilized regularly and kept in a light but not sunny position in the house or greenhouse. They require a winter minimum temperature of 50°F (10°C). Off-sets are produced fairly close in the leaf axils before and after flowering and are quite easily detached to root in peat and sand during the summer.

T. anceps. This is a 1 ft (30 cm) rosette of green leaves striped with fine brown lines at the base. The pink and green head of bracts is very similar to *T. lindenii* (below), but the blue flowers are only 1 in. (2.5 cm) across. White-flowered plants are sometimes seen. It will accept a little more shade than most species.

T. flabellata. This makes a rosette about 1 ft (30 cm) across, the narrow leaves green with silvery undersides and the flower head consisting of 8 to 12 separate spikes from a central stem, held above the leaves. Each spike is a brilliant orange, spear-shaped bract head and violet flowers with yellow anthers appear from the edges. The spike remains in colour for four to six weeks.

T. lindenii (*T. cyanea*). This popular plant is a 1 ft (30 cm) rosette of red-brown leaves, silver-scaled beneath. The central flower spike is a flat spearhead shape, a wax-like bract of pink and green from the edges of which bright blue 2 in. (5 cm) flowers emerge one after another, each lasting only two or three days, but the whole blooming for about a month in early summer (see p.146).

Tillandsia crocata has its silver-grey leaves so tightly curled in as to be almost cylindrical (see p.148)

Above left: *Tillandsia fasciculata* is a variable species from Colombia and Peru, having simple or multiple flower spikes.
Above right: *Tillandsia stricta* (see p.148).
Below left: Strong-growing *Tillandsia tenuifolia* withstands low temperatures.
Below right: *Tillandsia bergerii* has grey-scaled leaves

Tillandsia multicaulis is a soft-leaved species, one of the few to produce several flower spikes at once

SOFT-LEAVED PLANTS

Finally, there are the soft-leaved *Tillandsia* originating from moist tropical forests. Some species and hybrids of this group are being introduced here as houseplants by European growers. In cultivation, they need shade and a temperature of 60°F (15°C) and should be watered and fed in the same way as other shade-loving bromeliads like *Nidularium* and *Vriesea*. They generally produce a good number of offsets from the leaf axils after flowering, which may be rooted individually in 3 in. (7.5 cm) pots of peat and sand during the summer, when the temperature is not likely to fall below 68°F (20°C), or at any time of year in a heated propagator.

T. leiboldiana. This makes a rosette 1 to 1½ ft (30–45 cm) across of 20 to 30 soft green leaves, sometimes dark at the base and speckled with maroon. The upright branched spike of vermilion-red bracts holding lilac flowers is long-lasting and wax-like in appearance.

Other soft-leaved plants have simple or compound flower heads, as in *Racinea*, a recently created genus segregated from *Tillandsia*. *Racinea multicaulis* is a good example, with showy red bracts and yellow or violet flowers.

153

Aechmea

Aechmeas constitute a large genus of bromeliads and are widely distributed in nature from Mexico to Argentina. Nearly all of them form strong open rosettes, often retaining water in the centre of the plant. They have good root systems, which not only anchor them to their hosts – for they are mostly epiphytic – but take in sustenance from the rotting detritus that accumulates in pockets on the trees where they grow. The flower heads are very showy and remain so over a long period, although each individual floret lasts only a day or two. The flowers may be white, yellow, pink, red or purple and emerge from brilliantly coloured bracts, often of a different colour. Berried fruits are produced after flowering and these are usually highly coloured and last for several months.

Aechmeas are all very easy to grow and are excellent house-plants, able to accept the low humidity that generally prevails indoors. They are best given a light position in normal living-room conditions, where they will grow throughout the year. This means that they need to be watered in winter and summer and fed with a high potash fertilizer at every third watering. Quite small pots may be used for bromeliads relative to the size of the plant, the main criteria being to ensure stability. For most of the smaller Aechmea, forming a rosette up to 1½ ft (45 cm) diameter, a 5 in. (12.5 cm) clay pot or a 5½ in. (14 cm) plastic half-pot is sufficient and a compost of equal volumes of moss peat and coarse sand is suitable.

In the greenhouse, the same compost may be used for plants grown in pots and they should be positioned to receive as much light as possible, but without direct sunlight shining on them through the glass. A winter minimum temperature of 45°F (7°C) will do for the stiff-leaved kinds, if they are kept fairly dry, and applies in the descriptions below unless otherwise stated. However, those like Aechmea fulgens and A. 'Foster's Favorite', which have thinner, more flexible leaves, require 50°F (10°C) or more. All can be grown on a bromeliad tree.

The Brazilian species Aechmea fulgens has florets which turn from violet to red as they age (see p.157)

155

Above: *Aechmea fasciata*, the popular urn plant, may be grown on into a multi-headed specimen after flowering
Below left: the vivid flower head of *Aechmea chantinii* persists for several weeks
Below right: *Aechmea cylindrata* is very free flowering in summer

After flowering, most *Aechmea* produce their offsets on strong woody stolons, often several inches long. This allows the development of new rosettes without congestion if a specimen multi-headed plant is wanted (see p.138), or the offsets may be detached and potted as separate plants (see p.141).

A. chantinii. This beautiful Amazonian species consists of an open rosette of about a dozen leaves, which are 2 in. (5 cm) broad and 1 ft (30 cm) long, decorated with broad bands of green and white. In August it bears a dense panicle of red and yellow flowers surrounded by bright red bracts. Sometimes available from florists, it is a good houseplant but should have a winter minimum temperature of 60°F (15°C).

A. cylindrata. This has a long cylindrical flower spike in June, up to 9 in. (23 cm) long and 2 in. (5 cm) in diameter, of rose-pink bracts enclosing pale blue flowers, which are followed by long-lasting pink berries. It is one of the smaller *Aechmea*, with a rosette 1½ ft (45 cm) in diameter, comprising firm green leaves edged with small brown spines. It comes from Brazil.

A. fasciata. Probably the best known member of the genus is the urn plant, which forms an open rosette 2 ft (60 cm) across of very stiff, grey-green, spine-edged leaves, banded with silver-grey. The leaves are 2 to 3 in. (5–7.5 cm) wide and form a central cup or vase which will retain water. The flower head rises from the centre of the rosette to make a stiff, rather solid-looking arrangement of light purple flowers surrounded by prickly pink bracts and bract leaves. This showy flower spike lasts for several months under a wide range of temperatures, from 45°F (7°C) to 100°F (37°C) (see p.187).

A. 'Foster's Favorite'. This is one of the most popular hybrids, with about 20 narrow, glossy, wine-red leaves 1 ft (30 cm) long, slightly recurving to form a small rosette. The drooping panicle of blue and orange flowers appears in summer, later giving way to coral-red berries. It should have a minimum winter temperature of 50°F (10°C). There is also a variegated form with stripes of white along the leaf blades, but, like most variegated bromeliads, it is not easy to obtain since plants must be propagated by offsets (see p.159).

A. fulgens. This Brazilian species has a large spike of violet flowers contained in bright orange-red bracts. The florets turn red as they age and are succeeded by round, red, shining berries. It is one of the soft-leaved types, with 1 ft (30 cm) leaves, green on top and with a grey wax-like coating underneath. The variety *discolor* has dark wine-red leaves. A temperature of 50°F (10°C) is necessary in winter and rather less light than for most aechmeas (see p.154).

A. gamosepala. A tough rosette of 1 ft (30 cm) leaves, greyish below and tinged at the base with black-purple, this is one of the easiest aechmeas to grow. The flower is an open spike of rose-pink and blue in June and July, followed by round pink berries, the whole held well above the leaves.

A. nudicaulis. This is one of the aechmeas that form tall upright tubes. The few leaves are 1 to 3 ft (30–90 cm) high, depending on the particular clone, with strong black spines on the edges. The flower spike, produced in May, is a long-lasting cylindrical head of bright yellow flowers cupped in brilliant red stem bracts. It is very free-flowering and produces offsets on strong prickly stolons (see p.158).

A. orlandiana. This Brazilian species forms a stiff upright rosette of yellow-green leaves cross-banded with dark brown. It requires more warmth in winter than many aechmeas.

Above left: *Aechmea nudicaulis* (see p.157) remains showy for a long period
Above right: The hybrid *Aechmea* 'Royal Wine'
Below left: *Aechmea weilbachii* var. *leodiensis* is a soft-leaved plant
Below right: *Aechmea orlandiana*

A. pineliana. This Central American species is a rosette about 2 ft (60 cm) across, with dark green leaves banded silver below and with black spines on their edges. The dense spike of yellow flowers is surrounded by bright red bracts, while the floral bracts have light brown bristles at their tips, giving a teazle-like appearance. The leaves will become red in a good light, particularly at flowering time, which is usually May or June.

A. 'Royal Wine'. A soft-leaved plant, this generally produces its flowers in summer, followed by long-lasting berries. Offsets are freely borne on stolons. It should have a winter temperature of 50°F (10°C).

A. weilbachii var. leodiensis. The soft green leaves are often tinted with maroon-red. It likes a minimum temperature of 55°F (13°C) and will flower in fairly shady conditions.

OTHER SPECIES AND RELATED PLANTS

Many other species of *Aechmea* are seen in collections and at shows, but, before being tempted to buy an unknown plant, you should find out its ultimate size; some may grow to 3 ft (90 cm) or more in diameter and could become an embarrassment in a small greenhouse or home. Other plants related to *Aechmea* are encountered from time to time, such as *Hohenbergia*, *Portea* and *Streptocalyx*, the latter now reclassified within *Aechmea*. These too tend to be rather large for the average grower and mostly require a winter temperature of 60°F (15 °C).

Aechmea 'Foster's Favorite' is a popular hybrid, propagated by offsets (see p.157)

Billbergia

Billbergias are closely allied to *Aechmea* and need the same cultural treatment as the hard-leaved members of that genus, like *Aechmea fasciata*. Their distribution in nature is through Central America from southern Mexico to Argentina and they are usually found as epiphytes, growing into large clumps in open situations near the edge of forests, where they receive strong light. Most species form stiff, upright, cylindrical tubes, in contrast to the open rosettes of aechmeas, and need as much light as possible short of scorching. The leaves are tough, edged with strong spines, often banded with silver-grey and, in some cases, blotched and marbled with red and white as well. The flower spikes are striking, in shades of blue, green and yellow, shown off by large pink or red stem bracts. Unlike *Aechmea*, the flowers are comparatively short-lived, lasting only one or two weeks. Nearly all species have a definite flowering time, most of them blooming in the spring.

Almost without exception, billbergias will stand a temperature of 45°F (7°C) in the winter, if kept dry, and they are equally at home in pots or on a bromeliad tree, in the home, conservatory or greenhouse. During the summer months, most of them can be put outside in a lightly shaded position, where the colour of the leaves is enhanced, with many developing a strong red tinge.

After flowering, most *Billbergia* produce their offsets quite close to the parent plant. The easiest way to remove them is to tip the whole plant out of its pot and tease away the soil around the base. The pups can then be detached readily with a sideways and downwards pressure, while the old plant may be repotted to produce more offsets. The pups are potted into a sand and moss peat mixture in 3 in. (7.5 cm) pots. Water them only when the compost is dry and they should flower the following season.

B. amoena. This Brazilian species is a stiff tubular plant about 1½ ft (45 cm) tall and 2 in. (5 cm) in diameter. The green leaves, suffused with red and marbled with cream, have distinct silver bands across them and small brown spines at the edges. The upright spike carries a few yellow-green flowers margined with blue, set off by several large pink bracts, appearing in January or February. The offsets grow close

Billbergia pyramidalis var. *pyramidalis* flowers low down in the centre, unlike most other plants in the genus (see p.162)

161

to the parent plant on very short, thick stolons and may be left so that the plant makes a clump.

B. chlorosticta. Known to gardeners for many years as *B. saundersii*, this has slightly arching, narrow 1½ ft (45 cm) leaves of brownish green, with copious cream-white spotting and banding when grown in a good light. It forms an upright rosette, from the centre of which the slightly drooping flower spike is produced in May, with bright red stem bracts and a large panicle of red and violet flowers. Offsets grow quite close to the parent as in *B. nutans* and, like them, should flower after one season of growth.

B. 'Muriel Waterman'. The stout tubular rosette, about 3 in. (7.5 cm) in diameter, opens out to a funnel at the top of some six to eight leaves. These are rose-maroon with transverse silver bands, making it one of the most colourful foliage billbergias. The showy flower spike has pink bracts and yellow flowers edged with steel-blue.

B. nutans. Probably the most commonly grown bromeliad, this will survive almost freezing temperatures if it is dry. It flowers regularly in spring, bearing a drooping spike of yellow-green flowers edged with blue. The stem carries several deep pink, papery bracts below the flower head. The tufted rosette is made up of about 15 grey-green, narrow, tapering leaves 1½ ft (45 cm) long. Offsets produced on short stolons root easily.

B. porteana. One of a distinct group of billbergias whose flowers have tightly coiled petals. It is tall, up to 3 ft (90 cm), forming a tube 3 in. (7.5 cm) in diameter of six to eight leaves, recurving slightly at the tips, dull green, mealy-banded on the back and edged with spines. The flower stem, appearing in August, is about as tall as the leaves and carries several 6 in. (15 cm) bright red bracts, while the drooping panicle is up to 1 ft (30 cm) long, with green flowers margined in violet. These are followed by large ridged ovaries covered with silver-grey wool, which last several months and usually give fertile seed. Seeds may be sown to produce flowering plants in three years. Offsets generally take two years to flower.

B. pyramidalis. This Brazilian species flowers low in the centre of the rosette. The flower head, pink and purple, is enclosed in an open flattish rosette of grey-green leaves, each 2 in. (5 cm) wide, 10 in. (25 cm) long, with blunt tips. Offsets are produced on strong 4 to 6 in. (10–15 cm) stolons; if not removed, a plant can soon cover a large area. The variety *concolor* has pale green, glossy leaves and a central flower head of 'dayglo' pink.

QUESNELIA

These are very similar to *Billbergia*, forming somewhat stiff, upright rosettes and being just as easy to grow. However, most *Quesnelia* have spine-edged, spine-tipped leaves and are thus less attractive as houseplants. The species most often seen is *Q. liboniana*. It is a narrow, few-leaved, upright tube, 1½ ft (45 cm) tall, with spine-edged grey-green leaves. The flower spike has a red stem and blue and red flowers in April, sometimes followed by orange-yellow berries. The pups form at the ends of long, very spiny stolons.

Above and below: *Quesnelia liboniana*, from Brazil, is the commonest species of this genus and was the first to be introduced, in the mid-nineteenth century

Cryptanthus

The Cryptanthus species and hybrids have earned the name of earth stars on account of their shape. They make very flat rosettes of 10 to 30 tapering pointed leaves that hug the ground, varying in size from the 3 in. (7.5 cm) diameter of Cryptanthus roseus to the 2 ft (60 cm) of C. fosterianus and its hybrids. They are excellent houseplants for warm rooms and the smaller species are widely used in bottle gardens, where they will outlive most other plants without increasing in size too much (see also the Wisley Handbook, Houseplants, for information about bottle gardens). In the greenhouse earth stars need a winter minimum temperature of 60°F (15°C). In nature they are inhabitants of Brazil, growing in rich leafy material on the forest floor, and in cultivation they should therefore be given a similar, rich, open compost. A mixture of well-rotted leafmould, coarse sand and moss peat in equal volumes seems to suit them, enabling the roots to remain damp but not wet for most of the time. The amount of light required depends on the particular species and some need fairly heavy shade to bring out the best colours. Light is an important factor in determining their colours, so it is well worth experimenting to obtain the appearance that you prefer.

All earth stars produce small white flowers in the central leaf axils, mostly in summer. These are quite short-lived and soon wither away, while tiny new plants emerge. The pups grow very quickly and are easily detached to form new plants (see p.143).

C. acaulis. This small species is happier in fairly strong light, where it grows into a rosette about 3 in. (7.5 cm) across, consisting of a dozen or so leaves, red-brown, stiff and wavy-edged, with many tiny grey scales on their surface. It survives drier conditions than many other earth stars.
C. bivittatus. Frequently grown, particularly in bottle gardens, this is one of the smaller species. It forms a rosette of 15 to 25 leaves, 2 to 3 in. (5–7.5 cm) long and tapering to a point, with the edges waved and spined. In shade, the leaves are yellow-green with central and marginal stripes of dark green; in stronger light, they are tinged with bright pink, particularly at the base; and in bright light, the whole plant becomes reddish pink.
C. beuckerii. Growing a rosette about 4 in. (10 cm) across, this rather upright plant has unusual paddle-shaped leaves marbled in green and brown. It is happiest in shade. Offsets are produced in the leaf axils on short stolons.

Cryptanthus bromelioides var. tricolor, sometimes called the rainbow plant, should be grown in plenty of light to produce the best colours (see p.167)

Above: *Cryptanthus zonatus* is a medium-sized plant with decorative spine-edged leaves
Below: *Cryptanthus beuckerii* loves shade and has unusual paddle-shaped leaves (see p.165)

C. bromelioides. This is more upright in growth than most members of the genus, and has stiff, tapering, recurving, brown leaves produced at short intervals up a rigid stem, with a total spread of about 1 ft (30 cm). The species itself is not very often seen, but the variety *tricolor* is a popular houseplant. In this, the leaves are beautifully variegated with longitudinal stripes of green, brown and cream and shaded bright pink over much of the surface. It needs strong light to bring out the best colours. A peculiarity seems to be its extreme shyness of flowering, although offsets are freely produced from the leaf axils throughout the year (see p.164).
C. 'Cascade'. This American hybrid with bright red-brown leaves requires strong light. It is best grown in a hanging basket, since the 8 in. (20 cm) diameter rosette produces offsets on long stolons, not easily detached.
C. fosterianus. This is one of the largest species, sometimes attaining 2 ft (60 cm) across. To reach this size, it really needs a minimum temperature of 70°F (21°C) and a very rich compost. However, it will easily grow to 1 ft (30 cm) in diameter with 60°F (15°C). The dozen or so long tapering leaves that comprise the rosette are mainly red-brown, adorned with numerous zig-zag silver bands across the face, and are very stiff, almost artificial-looking. Like all *Cryptanthus*, it is a good plant for a bromeliad tree. There are many hybrids of this zebra-like species.
C. roseus. This small earth star delights in a shady position. It makes a rosette of 20 to 30 very narrow, pointed, wavy-edged leaves in a delicate cafe-au-lait colour, shaded pink at their bases. The rosette is 3 in. (7.5 cm) across, long-lasting and, with its many leaves, producing a large number of offsets which are easily grown on.
C. zonatus. This Brazilian species has broad, very stiff, wavy leaves with striking zebra-like banding. There are a number of varieties with different-coloured leaves, including *viridis*, green with silver bands, and *fuscus*, red-brown with silver bands. All need good light and a minimum winter temperature of 55°F (13°C).

×CRYPTBERGIA

Cryptanthus have been crossed with *Billbergia* and the resulting hybrids are intermediate in habit between the two genera. One of the commonest in cultivation is × *Cryptbergia rubra*. It forms a stiff rosette about 9 in. (23 cm) across of 20 to 30 hard, recurving, tapering leaves, glossy mahogany-red on top, silvery grey beneath. The dense stemless flower head in the centre of the plant has the yellow and blue flowers of *Billbergia nutans* and lasts a week in colour. Offsets are produced on short stolons and root easily, to flower in one year. It likes a peat and sand compost, with regular feeding at every third watering, and very bright light – almost full sun. A temperature of 45°F (7°C) does not trouble this plant at all.

Neoregelia

This is a genus of light-loving plants, mainly inhabitants of Brazil and epiphytic in nature, which have fairly stiff leaves, often with red marbling. There are numerous sports of some species, in particular of N. meyendorffii, with longitudinal bands of white or cream along the leaves. They are tank-forming, that is to say, the rosettes hold water in the cup formed by the leaves at the centre of the plant. The flowers are generally pink to purple, massed in a head nestling in the centre of the rosette – hence the common name of bird's nest for this group of bromeliads.

The many florets in a single flower head open two or three at a time over a period of several weeks, each one lasting only a day or two. Neoregelias are remarkable in that, just before flowering and often for several months, the whole central area of the plant becomes coloured, usually in a shade of red, being brightest at the base of the leaves and suffusing much of the leaf surface.

After flowering, offsets are mostly produced on stolons from the leaf axils, allowing plenty of room for new rosettes to develop. This is especially noticeable with the dwarf, more tubular, rosette-forming species, where a new plant may arise on a long thin stolon some distance from the parent, giving a very spidery appearance to a mature clump.

Neoregelias are easy plants to grow in the house or greenhouse, in pots or on a bromeliad tree. They should be placed in good light, but avoiding direct sunlight. Water them only when the compost is dry, feed with a high potash fertilizer at every third watering and, if the central cup is allowed to retain water in the summer, make sure that this is flushed out every couple of weeks to prevent stagnation. A suitable potting compost is composed of equal volumes of coarse sand and moss peat.

Winter temperatures of 45°F (7°C) will satisfy them if they are kept dry during the coldest periods. Offsets usually take two years to flower.

Above: Neoregelia meyendorffii var. variegata
Below: The fingernail plant Neoregelia spectabilis (see p.170)

N. concentrica. A Brazilian species, this attains 1½ ft (45 cm) across and has broad, dark green leaves and mauve colouring in the central area at flowering time. It requires the same treatment as *N. meyendorffii*.

N. fosteriana. This forms a thin, tubular, upright rosette of yellow-green leaves banded with light brown and slightly reflexed at the top. The bird's nest of mauve flowers is produced deep in the tube of leaves and offsets grow at the ends of long wiry stolons.

N. marmorata. This species has a rosette composed of up to 30 fairly stiff leaves, 1 ft (30 cm) long, which are green marbled with red-brown and turn brilliant red when the flower head is produced. It should be given as much light as possible for the most vivid colour. The offsets appear on stolons about 2 in. (5 cm) long and take two years to flower.

N. meyendorffii (*N. carolinae*). Grown from seed to flower in two to three years and produced in thousands for the houseplant market, this tough, almost people-proof plant is widely used for interior decoration in homes, foyers and shopping arcades. In flower, it is an open rosette of green leaves, 1¼ to 1½ ft (38–45 cm) in diameter, with the whole central area a brilliant wax-like red, enclosing the bird's nest flower head of mauve florets. The variegated leaf forms are spectacular and are quite readily available, even though they must be propagated by offsets (see pp.139 and 168).

N. spectabilis. The fingernail plant, as it is called, has purplish brown leaves with silver-grey lines across the backs and bright pink tips. They form a semi-open rosette about 1 ft (30 cm) across, but do not change colour at flowering time. The bird's nest flowers are blue. One of the hardiest species, it is best grown in strong light (see p.168).

N. tigrina. This species grows new plants at the end of long stolons and resembles *N. tristis* (below) in shape, but is even smaller. It has tiny tubular rosettes ¾ in. (2 cm) in diameter with slightly flaring tips. The leaves are shining green, banded heavily with mahogany.

N. tristis. Although of similar colouring to *N. marmorata* (above), this has a quite different rosette. About 10 leaves make a narrow tubular base, which rises to a height of 5 in. (12.5 cm) and then opens at the top to 6 in. (15 cm) across. The bird's nest head of blue flowers is sunk deep in the tube. New rosettes are produced on long thin stolons and often develop roots in mid-air. It is a particularly good plant for a bromeliad tree, climbing by means of the long stolons.

Nidularium

This small genus from Brazil is often confused with *Neoregelia*, owing to the similarity of the bird's nest type of flower head. In *Nidularium*, however, this is surrounded by coloured bracts and the whole assembly is a distinct separate entity on its own stem, rather than being buried in the rosette. A further notable difference is that the true leaves of the rosette do not colour as they do in *Neoregelia*.

Nidularium form open rosettes of broad flexible leaves, most in the range of 1 to 2 ft (30–60 cm) in diameter, and have bird's nest flower heads of white or purple flowers with a collar of brilliantly coloured bract leaves. The rather soft texture of the leaves indicates that the plants need a significant amount of shade and they do not like temperatures below 50°F (10°C).

The potting compost can be the usual sand and moss peat mixture which is suitable for most bromeliads. Regular feeding is required throughout the period of growth and should also continue after flowering. This will provide food for the production of offsets, which mostly develop close in the leaf axils. Like other bromeliads, each species of *Nidularium* has its own particular flowering time. The pups can take either one or two years to reach flowering size.

Since these bromeliads grow and flower in quite shady positions, they make excellent houseplants. In the home, water them only when the compost is dry and site them well away from a source of heat, such as a fire or radiator. They will then be very rewarding plants, maintaining a good shape and not becoming drawn as so many other plants do in shade. In the greenhouse, make sure that they are well shaded and certainly do not give them direct sunlight. A north-facing conservatory is ideal, perhaps in the company of foliage begonias, ferns and shade-loving plants with which these bromeliads will form an attractive display.

N. billbergioides. This is an upright rosette, about 1 ft (30 cm) high, of glossy, light green leaves 1 in. (2.5 cm) wide. The flower spike rises above the leaves and consists of white flowers 2 in. (5 cm) across, enclosed in bright yellow bracts which last for about six weeks. After flowering, the offsets grow on stolons 3 to 4 in. (7.5–10 cm) long. There are varieties with bracts of different colours, ranging from pale yellow to very dark red. This plant is frequently offered in shops and makes an excellent houseplant in most conditions.

Nidularium billbergioides is unusual in having the flower head on a long stalk
(see p.171)

N. burchellii. This nidularium is distinct from all other species. The rather upright
rosette is made up of 10 to 12 leaves, which are dull green above, purple below,
reflexing at the ends and 10 in. (25 cm) long. The flower head is held just above the
leaves and is made up of white flowers and small green bracts, the whole being
almost globular in shape and usually appearing in the late autumn. As the flowers
fade, they are then replaced by green berries, which will soon turn bright orange
and remain colourful for several months and well into the new year. It is a very
showy little plant. New plants develop at the end of wiry stolons 3 to 6 in. (7.5–15 cm)
long and root to flower the next year.

N. terminale This is a stemless species with a habit similar to *N. billbergioides*. The
rich, dark green leaves, sometimes blushed reddish, may reach $3\frac{1}{2}$ ft (1 m) long once
they reach maturity. Leaves are edged with dark brown teeth. The bright red scape
bracts enclose pale blue flowers. This species is usually rather variable.

N. fulgens. This is a rosette about 1 ft (30 cm) in diameter, which is rather more upright than most species, of pale green, glossy leaves slightly marbled with darker
green. The brilliant flower head lasts some weeks.

Nidularium regelioides is a 2 ft (60 cm) rosette of leathery leaves with red flowers. It needs a fairly shady position

N. innocentii. This is an open rosette of 30 or so leaves, which are green on the upper surface, dark purple underneath. The rosettes reach a diameter of $1\frac{1}{2}$ ft (45 cm) and form a water-retaining cup in the centre. At flowering time a bird's nest head of white flowers develops, and this is surrounded by stiff red-purple bracts. There are several varieties of this species, with the leaves being plain green or variously striped all the way along their length with white or cream.

Vriesea and Guzmania

Vriesea and *Guzmania* are mostly inhabitants of rain forests in Central and South America. They are similar in appearance, forming fairly open rosettes of soft leaves, and in their requirements, needing light shade and a winter minimum temperature of 60°F (15°C). They are grown from seed in large numbers in Europe for sale as houseplants, for which purpose they are superb, with long-lasting flower heads and often with coloured foliage. Although plants from 1 to 3 ft (30–90 cm) across or more are available, it is the smaller kinds that are generally offered. Most are grown in pots, using a rich free-draining compost: a mixture of equal volumes of leafmould, coarse grit or perlite and moss peat is suitable. Water when the compost is dry and feed with a liquid fertilizer at every third watering. Many of them have a water-retaining cup in the centre and, as mentioned earlier, this is best kept empty of water if they are grown as houseplants or if the temperature is likely to fall below 50°F (10°C).

V. carinata. A small Brazilian species some 8 in. (20 cm) across, this has a rosette made up of about 20 pale green, shiny leaves. The long-lasting flower spike is wax-like, with yellow flowers appearing from the edges of the red and yellow fan-shaped bract head in February or March. It will survive 50°F (10°C) in winter if the central cup is kept dry. After flowering, offsets are freely produced, which root easily and may be flowered in one year.

V. hieroglyphica. Often seen on sale, this is a beautiful plant with broad, glossy green leaves crossbanded with many irregular, fine brown lines. It grows quickly under warm conditions, but takes several years to reach flowering size. By this time, it is a rosette some 3 ft (90 cm) across, with 50 or 60 leaves, and needs a fair amount of space. The flower spike is 3 ft (90 cm) high, carrying tubular green bracts with yellow flowers.

V. rodigasiana. When not in flower, this plant is similar in size and shape to V. *carinata* (above). However, the spike is an upright stem 1 ft (30 cm) high, with single, cylindrical, bright yellow, waxen bracts at intervals up it, from which are produced large yellow flowers. The spike remains colourful for several weeks. Many pups appear after flowering and take two years to flower.

V. splendens. The flaming sword is commonly seen, either as a plant in flower or as a small seedling for use in bottle gardens. A small 4 in. (10 cm) plant is normally about a year old from seed and will need a further two years of growth to reach flowering size. A plant in flower is a rosette some 1 ft (30 cm) in diameter, with a

---

Vriesea carinata is an undemanding plant suitable for a bromeliad tree

Above: *Vriesea hieroglyphica* (see p.175) is an excellent foliage houseplant
Below left: The hybrid *Vriesea* 'Mariae' has bright green leaves
Below right: The hybrid 'Polonia' has a branched flower spike

Above: *Guzmania* 'Memoria' is very similar to *G. lingulata* but with red bracts
Below: *Guzmania sanguinea* may have red, orange or yellow bracts

central flower stem carrying a flat spear-like bract head of shining orange-red, from the edges of which yellow flowers emerge one at a time over a period of four to six weeks. The leaves are very ornamental, 2 in. (5 cm) wide and green with broad, irregular, brown bands. Recently developed hybrids have more brilliantly coloured leaves and some have flower spikes with branched stems, each carrying a coloured spearhead. These hybrids, like the species itself, usually produce only one offset after flowering and plants obtained are generally grown from seed.

V. tessellata (*V. gigantea*). This has ornamental foliage of blue-green with fine yellow-brown markings, but grows fairly large, some 3 ft (90 cm) high and wide, and takes several years to reach flowering size.

G. lingulata. One of the commonest guzmanias, this forms a 10 in. (25 cm) rosette of pale green, glossy, slightly reflexing leaves, from the centre of which rises a stout stem carrying a head of white flowers surrounded by brilliant yellow bracts. There are also varieties with orange or red bracts, the red-bracted ones often having red toning in the leaves. Commercially, they are grown from seed to flower in two years. Offsets are freely produced after flowering, which root quickly to flower the next season. A winter temperature of 50°F (10°C) will suit them, with light shading. They are very accommodating houseplants.

G. monostachya. This is a rosette of bright, pale green, 1 ft (30 cm) long leaves. The strong upright flower head is cylindrical, pointed at the top, with red, black and green bracts and white flowers. It requires a temperature of 60°F (15°C) in winter, with a little shade, and is summer-flowering.

G. musaica. As a foliage plant, this is very effective indoors, with its broad green leaves crossbanded with brown to form a rosette about 2 ft (60 cm) across. The flower spike is a compact, somewhat rounded head of orange-yellow inflated bracts with large, pale yellow flowers. It likes fairly heavy shade and a winter temperature of 60°F (15°C). Offsets are rather sparingly produced after flowering, so most plants are raised from seed, the seedlings taking three years to reach flowering size.

G. zahnii. This is a larger plant, growing to 3 ft (90 cm) across, with broad, yellowish-green leaves, striped with fine maroon lines on the undersides and red at their bases. The upright flower spike consists of red and yellow flowers and very large, reflexing, red bracts. It comes from Costa Rica and needs a temperature of 60°F (15°C) in winter. It is a striking plant in flower and has been the parent of many showy hybrids used as houseplants. It may be propagated by offsets during the summer months (see p.140).

Guzmania lingulata var. *cardinalis* has red bracts

Terrestrial Bromeliads

As opposed to the majority of epiphytic bromeliads, some are found as true terrestrials growing in the ground, generally in open country where they receive maximum light. Many are fairly large and armed with fierce spines and are not really suitable as house-plants. A cool greenhouse is the best abode for most of them, where they would associate well with desert cacti.

ANANAS

The best known and most important of the terrestrials is the pine-apple, *Ananas comosus*, which has become naturalized in many tropical regions of the world. There are numerous subspecies and varieties with various sizes and shapes of fruit and different foliage, including attractive variegated leaf forms. All need similar treatment, with as much light and heat as possible.

To root a pineapple top from a bought fruit, choose the warmest time in summer. Remove the small rosette from the top of the fruit and cut away any residual pineapple flesh. Take off some of the lower leaves to leave a short woody stem base and allow this to dry off for two or three days. Then pot it into a mixture of equal volumes of moss peat and coarse sand to come just up to the bottom of the remaining leaves, in a 4 in. (10 cm) pot. Water it in, do not cover with a polythene bag and keep it in as a warm a place as possible, where it will get maximum light – on a shelf by a window, for instance, or near the glass in a greenhouse. Water only when the compost has become dry, bearing in mind that this will happen quickly in the warm light conditions. In summer, roots should begin to form in four to six weeks and, when this occurs, a high potash fertilizer like Tomorite may be added to the water at every third watering. Once the plant starts to produce new leaves from the top, it will have quite a strong root system and will need potting on into a 6 in. (15-cm) pot, using a rich compost of equal volumes of moss peat, sand and well-rotted garden compost. It must then be grown in the warmest place possible, certainly not less than 60°F (15°C) in winter, with maximum light, even direct sunlight.

One of the many forms of the pineapple, *Ananas comosus* var. *variegatus*

On average, a pineapple grows to 3 ft (90 cm) or so in diameter, with very tough, spine-edged leaves, and may well produce fruit after two or three years. It then has a manner of growth like other bromeliads and will give offsets from the leaf axils, which are rooted more easily than fruit tops. Offsets are sometimes produced from around the tuft of leaves on the top of the fruit and these may also be used for increase.

BROMELIA

Similar in growth to the pineapple and making large plants with very spiny, stout, recurved leaves are members of the genus *Bromelia*, which is native to tropical-subtropical South America. The flower spike is usually red and purple and forms a brilliant head of colour in the centre of the rosette, followed by yellow or orange berries. They are very striking in flower, but tend to become too large for the average greenhouse or home. Treatment is the same as for the pineapple.

FASCICULARIA

Another genus with extremely spiny leaves and growing rather too big for pot culture is *Fascicularia*, from Chile. However, in the southwest of England and other mild districts, *Fascicularia bicolor* (see p.186) appears to be hardy and may develop into a clump several feet across, of rosettes formed from narrow, spine-edged, grey-green leaves. It blooms in summer with a dense central head of pale blue and red set low in the middle of each rosette, while many of the central leaves turn a brilliant sealing-wax red.

PUYA

The puyas, some of which attain a height of 30 ft (9 m) in the South American Andes, include a few which are just about manageable in pots. One of these, *Puya alpestris*, is usually grown from seed, which germinates readily (see p.143). The seedlings grow quickly, needing a temperature of only 40°F (5°C) after they are three or four months old, but requiring good light at all times and not too much water. As they grow, they make very dense rosettes of narrow, grey-green, recurving leaves, edged with numerous strong spines. At two years from seed, they ought to be in 5 in. (12.5 cm) pots and will have a leaf spread of about 2 ft (60 cm). If potted on into larger pots, they will get even bigger.

Kept in the same pot, the plants will eventually flower, which is worth waiting for, although it may take five or six years from seed. The tall flower stem bears a compound spike of large green and light blue flowers and pink bracts, the whole flower head lasting about a month. It is a xerophytic bromeliad, inhabiting areas where water is scarce and maximum light is received. In cultivation, therefore, water only when the compost is dry and feed with a high potash fertilizer about once a month.

ABROMEITIELLA

At the other end of the size scale is *Abromeitiella brevifolia* (see p.186), a xerophytic bromeliad from Argentina and Bolivia. It forms a large mound of tiny rosettes, each 2 in. (5 cm) in diameter, with stiff, grey-green, spiny 1 in. (2.5 cm) leaves and greenish white flower heads set among them. Its growth is very much like that of the cushion-forming saxifrages. Frost-free conditions are necessary for this little bromeliad, with as much light as possible and very little water.

DYCKIA and HECHTIA

These two genera require similar culture. The succulent-looking *Dyckia sulphurea* (*D. brevifolia*) has a rosette of 20 to 30 leaves, 4 to 5 in. (10–12.5 cm) long and tapering to a point, very thick and rigid with tiny toothed spines on the edges, pale green on top and silver with green lines beneath. The 1 to 1¼ ft (30–38 cm) stem bears eight to ten flowers spaced on the upper half, sulphur-yellow and wax-like. It is easily grown from seed to flower in about two years.

Hechtia argentea makes a dense mass of numerous rigid, silvery, spine-edged leaves up to 1½ ft (45 cm) long, finely scaled on the undersides. The flower spike is an open panicle of many small white flowers and light brown bracts. Like other xerophytic plants, it is easily grown in a peat and sand mixture with little water.

PITCAIRNIA

This large genus of bromeliads is not often seen outside specialist collections, even though some of the smaller ones can be grown easily in pots. Distributed in nature through Central and South America, they are nearly all terrestrial, with a few saxicolous and one or two epiphytic species. In appearance and cultivation needs, they may be divided into two groups.

Above: *Bromelia balansae* has a large semi-cylindrical inflorescence with whitish flowers, the fruits having the flavour of pineapple
Below: *Pitcairnia ferruginea*, the largest member of the genus, has long spine-edged leaves

In the first group are plants with soft, green, drooping, almost grass-like leaves, spineless and forming large tufted clumps with a strong root system. Since all like acid soil, a peat and sand mixture with the addition of some leafmould is a satisfactory compost. They may be grown in pots or planted in a greenhouse bed or border, with a winter minimum temperature of 50°F (10°C), in a light but not sunny location. Watering is required only when the compost becomes dry. Much growth is made during the summer months, when they should be fed with a high potash fertilizer at every other watering. During the inactive winter period, water only at monthly intervals. Spikes of red, yellow, orange or white flowers are produced in summer, lasting about two weeks.

One of the smaller species is *Pitcairnia andreana*, which has tufts of narrow leaves 9 in. (23 cm) high, light green above and grey below. The upright flower spike carries 10 to 12 large orange-yellow flowers in June. Many offsets are produced, whether the plant is in flower or not, and a dense clump soon results. This is easily divided, as the divisions already have roots. In addition, the plant is self-fertile and sets seed freely.

Similar in its grass-like habit, *Pitcairnia maidifolia* is up to 3 ft (90 cm) tall and has an erect flower spike of white flowers surrounded by red and green bracts in July. There are many other species of the same shape but with different flower heads.

The second group is typified by *Pitcairnia pungens*. This is rarely more than 1¼ ft (38 cm) high and forms a somewhat bulbous, very spiny base. The deciduous green leaves are armed with strong brown spines and vary in length from 1 to 12 in. (2.5–30 cm). In autumn, the leaves fall off, leaving a spined bulbous base which must have a completely dry rest period from November to April, with a winter minimum temperature of 50°F (10°C). Watering should commence only when new leaf growth has started. Soon after this happens, a spike of orange-red flowers appears from the top of the bulb and offsets are produced simultaneously. *Pitcairnia nigra* is like *P. pungens*, but has vermillion-red flowers. This and other similar species are normally found growing on rocks in nature and therefore need a very open, free-draining compost, consisting of two parts of coarse sand and one part of moss peat by volume. They need strong light at all times.

A few pitcairnias, mostly the very large species like *Pitcairnia ferruginea*, resemble puyas with their heavily spined leaves and are difficult to distinguish until the flowers are produced.

Above: *Fascicularia bicolor* (see p. 182) is one of the five species in this genus
Below: *Abromeitiella brevifolia* (see p. 183) needs frost free conditions, good
light and little water

Aechmea fasciata, the urn plant, with a long-lasting flower spike

Index

Page numbers in **bold** refer to illlustrations